BENGAL
Write Ahead

BENGAL
Write Ahead

Best 50 Stories on Bengal
from the Facebook Contest

Foreword by **DEREK O'BRIEN**

Edited and Compiled by **KOLKATA BLOGGERS**

Published by
Rupa Publications India Pvt. Ltd 2016
7/16, Ansari Road, Daryaganj
New Delhi 110002

Sales centres:
Allahabad Bengaluru Chennai
Hyderabad Jaipur Kathmandu
Kolkata Mumbai

Copyright © Kolkata Bloggers 2016

All rights reserved.
No part of this publication may be reproduced, transmitted,
or stored in a retrieval system, in any form or by any means,
electronic, mechanical, photocopying, recording or otherwise,
without the prior permission of the publisher.

ISBN: 978-81-29140-42-5

First impression 2016

10 9 8 7 6 5 4 3 2 1

The moral right of the author has been asserted.

Printed at Replika Press Pvt. Ltd, India

This book is sold subject to the condition that it shall not, by way of trade
or otherwise, be lent, resold, hired out, or otherwise circulated, without the
publisher's prior consent, in any form of binding or cover
other than that in which it is published.

Contents

Foreword	ix
Introduction	xiii
When You Think About Me Ishani Pant	1
Dickensian Dilemma Ashish Agarwal	4
Alzheimer Mehuli Saha Ray	7
Bengal: A Raucous Melody Meghna Roy	10
ঋতুদা.. তোমার জন্য.. Priyanka Chatterjee	13
A Literary Stroll Through Boi Para Kasturi Patra	15
God's Own Abode Rupsha Bhadra	18
'Bengoal' Right Ahead Arinjay Ghosh	21
The Idiosyncratic Collectivity Samuel Prateek Toppo	24
অনুরণন Sudipta Nath	27

Creative Flourish in Bengal Cinema Archita Mittra	29
Citius Altius Fortius Resham Das	32
West Bengal—It's Heart Over Head for the Residents Aviroop Mookherjee	35
My Tryst with Bangaliana Moyurie Som	38
বাঙাল ঘটি জমজমাটি Srijata Chatterjee	41
The Majestic Bong Mellows Gurbinder Kaur	43
The Rise of a New Bengal Madhutamo Sengupta	46
The Complete Package: West Bengal Rajni Shukla	49
Tumi Ashbe Boley Taai Nandini Nag	52
আনন্দ ধারা Sahel Ghosh	55
Parts of a Whole Suchisubhra Sarkar	57
Flavours of Festivity in Bengal Sourina Bose	60
The City of Joy Speaks Garima Behal	63
Life in a Metro Advika Jalan	66

"আমি আমার আমিকে চিরদিনই এই বাংলায় খুঁজে পাই...." Srija Gupta	69
Filming Bengal Aritra Basu	71
'She' Deepsikha Chowdhury	74
Kolkata's Affection Towards Durga Ma Sreoshi Bakshi	76
The Other Side of Stigma Monideepa Majumdar	79
Performing Arts of Bengal Probuddho Ganguly	81
Divine Dhaak Beat Manoj Kumar Tigga	84
'B' for BENGAL Sounak Sengupta	87
The Celebration of Home-coming Kasturi Patra	89
Bengal: A Land of Contradictions Aindrilla Chakraborty	92
বাংলার গান Sankhadeep Sengupta	95
Bengal Beckons You Indranil Roy	96
Chromatic Bengal Swastika Bandyopadhyay	99
Bengal—The Land of Culture Dahlia Ghosh	102

Bangla Gaan: A Buffet of Wonders Proiti Seal Acharya	104
Kolkata Prakalpa Bhattacharya	107
Where Dreams Grow! Tiasa Banerjee	109
Inspiration Aritra Basu	112
Requiem for the City of Joy Rajeswari Dasgupta	115
Torchbearer of Indian Cinema Sumanto Sengupta	118
ঝক্কাস Tandrima Bhattacharya Chatterjee	121
The Perfect Getaway Kanishka Chakrabarty	123
Chai Gorom Chai! Kasturi Dasgupta	125
Story of Football Sandeep Dutta	127
Bengal Always Ahead Suvadip Ghosh	130
সোহাগ Prabir Biswas	133

Foreword

To ask a person to write about his or her community—be it linguistic, racial or national—is to open the floodgates to memories, nostalgia, tales of achievement and failure. And to ask a person who has experienced Bengal to do so, is even more interesting. For a number of reasons, this part of India creates strong feelings among those who have known it or lived here.

The 'Bengal Write Ahead' contest was designed as a unique writing competition, where people could express their thoughts on Bengal in either English or Bengali. From the time the idea was conceptualized, I was looking forward to reading the articles that would be submitted online. There is so much that one can say about the state where I was born, grew up and now live. The geographical breadth and the diversity of its fauna. The lush green vegetation and the lowering storm clouds during the monsoon. The music. The art. The history. The festivals. The people who are passionate, argumentative, artistic.

I was delighted that Facebook kept the contest open to people from all over the world and for a wide range of ages. This ensured there would be a diversity of views and opinions. It also meant that the non-resident Bengali, the 'probashi', could also write. (I wonder if other communities have a word similar to 'probashi'. It implies that you may leave Bengal, but Bengal never really leaves you.)

Even though I did not get the opportunity to read all the entries, reading the top fifty pieces submitted to Facebook was a pleasure. In sentence after sentence, I could feel the passion. The love for music, films, food, sport, literature, festivals, Kolkata is so clearly expressed. There is so much one can write about my favourite city and it finds a place here. Many pieces talk about the personality of the people of Bengal—how they can argue with you while offering you the choicest piece of fish, how they spin words into beautiful literature and create works of art that are truly unique. There are some stories about the Kolkata Metro and the microcosmic slice of life it puts on view. Sport, particularly football and cricket, appear in the pages of this book evoking the magic of a match on the Maidan or the 'Mexican wave' at the Eden Gardens.

Kolkata and Bengal are the only places I can call home.

Bengal Write Ahead is more than a compilation of award-winning articles submitted to Facebook and shared around the world. It is a celebration of my state. My city.

My home. I invite you to explore Biswa Bangla through its pages.

Derek O'Brien
April 2016

P.S.: For conversations about Bengal and more, stay connected with me on Facebook at the URL http://www.facebook.com/MPDerekOBrien/ and on Twitter on my handle @quizderek.

Introduction

From 27 February to 12 March 2016, Facebook in partnership with Rupa Publications, Kolkata Bloggers and Red FM organized a writing contest called 'Bengal Write Ahead', which invited entrants to write within 500 words highlighting various aspects of Bengal.

The participants submitted stories, articles and posts on the state in English and Bengali and the topics covered music, books, performing arts, culture, events, recreation, politics, sport, education, health, industry, economy and infrastructure.

The writings touch upon varied facets like Bengali festivals, rankings of football teams, the artist of Kumortuli, industrial facilities of Bengal and more. Some writers spun the articles into the format of stories with plots and characters, while some chose to keep it informative.

We have been overwhelmed by the enthusiastic participation of so many people across the nation and outside, eager to highlight their positive emotions associated with Bengal. It is only with their continued support and encouragement that Bengal can remain as highly regarded and respected as it is today.

The top fifty stories, selected and judged by reputed names across the country, have been compiled into this book and top ten winners were awarded cash prizes. I would like to thank the judges Devapriya Roy, Arunava Sinha, Nivedita Sen, Sajni Mukerji and Saurav Jha for taking out time to read the pieces.

Bengal Write Ahead brings to you the best of Bengal's positive stories. Read on to discover fifty fresh outlooks about the state we all love and cherish.

Ankhi Das
Public Policy Director
Facebook India, South and Central Asia

When You Think About Me

Ishani Pant

WHEN YOU THINK about where you were born, the land that nurtured you and raised you, the essence of Bengal comes wafting back in languid waves like those hungry waves that lap at the fallen shore, in search of some fast fading truth; like the lonesome sun, craving always a taste of the salty sea breeze dancing with the sea. But most of all it is like the soporific songs mothers sing to their children before the water seeps through all their dreams.

You think of that one summer you spent in the Sundarbans, surrounded by nothing but green land and green marshes. A spot of Bengal, closer to the wild, residing in the thick gnarled roots of the mangroves. Here, the days melt into night and everything is still with the humidity of a thousand words. Boats linger on the stagnant waters, insignificant next to the vastness of this native sky. Your native sky. A strange, wonderful warmth spreads over these memories, the way thin jhol spreads over the white, misty rice on your plate during a family lunch on Sundays.

When you think about Bengal, specks of scattered lyrical sounds find their way to your rain soaked flat in Paikpara and you think about the city which flows through your veins. You think about the crowded streets of Kolkata where you often lost yourself among the infinite stalls of phuchkas and the overwhelmingly sweet scent of mishti shops. A city built of clusters of men and women in the metro, clusters of books resting in a corner of College Street, clusters of children falling over each other on the side of the road, and clusters of restless thoughts trapped inside your drowsy head during an afternoon nap.

A small smile plays on your lips as you think about the countless plays you watched at Nandan and the casual debates over a five-rupee cup of cha. You remember the winter days, when you strolled through the zoo, filled to the brim with picnicking families and how their pleasant bickering floated up towards the careless clouds.

When you think about Bengal, almost everything is masked with the faint scent of rain and the oppressive summer evenings turn into cool, blissful monsoon nights. The roaring kal baishaki rips through the trees and you wait for it to blow you away, content in the moment. Often, the rain is relentlessly romantic, and you fall like a little bird in love. It drips off your roof and windows, quietly filling the land, brushing away the distractions. The land only smiles and whispers to you. 'When you think about me,' it says, 'When you think about me...'

Dickensian Dilemma

Ashish Agarwal

IT IS COMMON knowledge that the rows of makeshift stalls, which stretch both sides of the narrow road aptly christened 'College Street', quintessentially serve as a safe haven for the atypical Bengali bibliophile. Characteristically 'North Kolkata', the sleepy slumber here is broken everyday with school and college students rushing to the sounds of the bells signalling the beginning of classes. As the local cha stall owner begins warming up the milk and cleaning his utensils, one hears a series of discordant sounds comprising keys being turned in locks, unfurling of wooden shafts and bundles of books dropping heavily. As the dust settles, one can now see a treasure trove of book spines gleaming in the morning sunlight. The cacophony of myriad sounds only grows louder to settle into an eventual status quo. The hand-pulled rickshaws still laden with various prints of the latest exam-help books with their master at the helm make way through the narrow bylanes struggling to make their voice heard and reach their destination as soon as possible.

Meanwhile, a steady stream of customers start trickling in—from school children with their parents in tow carrying their booklists, crossing them off as they visit one shop after another, to the kurta clad, bespectacled nomadic gentleman in search of that elusive perfect evening read. One can see the decision being made in a clear moment of epiphany as their search ends with their eyes resting upon the perfect cover and thereafter hear the heated consensus on the price.

A single shelf adorned with Tolstoy, Bukowski, Archer, Mills and Boon, et al, poses a serious dilemma to the reader. One could only imagine if such a dysfunctional combination were to meet in real life. Oh! what a spectacle it would be.

This is something rare. Such a culmination of culture and passion in this day and age. Where time stands still in a small geographical area, seemingly immune from the vagaries of the world and its people. A dose of nostalgia hits you like a whiff of the best brand of Scotch one lovingly preserves throughout one's lifetime. A potpourri of people, culture, tastes, smell, sights and sounds. Of discussions, ideas, notions, conjectures, theories and hypotheses. One can experience it all in this short span of 1,000 steps. Such is the magic of the city. Such is the resolve. Undeterred and unfettered. Refusing to bow down to society's ideas of progress, of conformity. Such is a world we have created. In this short stretch, one forgets the future, what is to be, what could be, instead, revelling in the present.

Alzheimer

Mehuli Saha Ray

THAKUMA BEGAN HER story for the day, with eleven-year-old Piku listening to her diligently. Once upon a time, there lived two simpletons, Gobinda, a distant descendant of Puru, and Anuti, a Sutaputri. After they got married, Anuti bore a girl. She named her Kali. When she grew up, it worried her parents, because she showed no signs of grace a maiden of her age should possess. She was tomboyish, and even puberty did not do any good to her. The other people mockingly called her Kikila.

'Kikila?' inquired Piku.

'Ask your Google. Don't disrupt the flow while I create, Piku.' Thakuma was seventy-four years old, and showing signs of Alzheimer's disease. While other members of the family considered what she said a part of her derangement, it intrigued Piku. He looked forward to the cool roasted mango juice, and to the visits to Behrampur.

Back to the story. They wondered who will marry her. But Kali was talented. She mastered the art of making limestone and coir, and digging canals to irrigate fields. Hence she even acquired the names Koli Kata, or Khal Kata. Sounds like Kolkata, Piku thought to himself. Due to her talents, the son of the village ruler, Shiraz, fell in love with her, but before he could act, a young British officer, Robert, proposed marriage to her. Kali fell for the white man, and her parents were relieved that she would not remain a spinster and earn a bad name in the community. But Robert had other plans.

He sold her to the British, who each used her for their own interests. Some burnt her with cigars, some starved her. She even developed Vitiligo (some white patches on her dark skin). They kept on diminishing her, in ways I cannot explain, Piku. Everyone claimed her. British, Nationalists, Leftist—everyone wanted to claim their portion in her already inflicted body. She tolerated everything, Piku, and never talked back, like your mother. Piku chuckled at the sudden reference, and remembered that Ma had asked him to finish his homework, or else she would not let him watch the IPL finals between Kolkata Knight Riders and Delhi Daredevils. 'Wait! I have homework to finish!' Piku declared and ran off. He finished it hastily, and rushed back to Thakuma, but she was asleep by then. So he decided to Google Kikila on Baba's phone. He read the entire Wikipedia article. Kikila was redirected to Kolkata. His hometown. The city with trams, Howrah bridge, teastall addas, political rallies. The city he loved, the city Thakuma loved. Her Alzheimer's disease bridged the gap between their generations.

He did not watch the match. Neither did he ask Thakuma the end of the story when she woke up, for he knew Delhi had won against Kolkata. And maybe someone had stolen Kali's splendor too. But everything melancholic was beautiful. Kali was beautiful. Kolkata is beautiful. He silently sipped his mango juice and looked at birds flying home in the dusk, while Thakuma massaged oil on his scalp.

Bengal: A Raucous Melody

Meghna Roy

'EVERY EVENING I sit by the stream staring at my own reflection on the opposite bank. Is that land so unlike me that we need to erect a wall in between? While I contemplate thus, I hear from the other side the distant sound of folk songs sung by exhilarated minstrels, and instantly recognize the tune. As I start humming it, it dawns on me that the tune resonates my heartbeats. It is not long before I get a feeling—a feeling that it is not after all parochialism to find the entire world embodied in your homeland. Bengal on both sides of the border is that music which keeps almost 253 million people going.'

The music produced in Bengal is as varied as its landscape. The depth of lyrics in Lalon Fakir's compositions, the intoxication in every tune by Moheener Ghoraguli, the immortal songs of Tagore which linger in the mind long after the music stops playing, is each a bead that adorns the land in a single string of harmony. Sanskrit chants heralded the music scene here as early as in the 13th century, eventually being carried forward by Vaishnav poetry. The cultural ethos of Bengal being an all-inclusive one, since the Middle Ages the land has nurtured Muslim and Hindu trends alike under the patronage of the Nawabs and the prosperous baro bhuiyas. The rhythmic sentence punctuated with a blend of devotional and carnal forms of love that Ramprasad Sen and Vidyapati commenced, finds complete expression in the quest for Moner Manush (the conscience) in the Baul tradition of the folk genre. Each milestone in the journey of music adds meaning to the entire picture.

If there is any form of music which accompanies us in every phase of life, be it in the contemplative hours of seeking Divine shelter, or the feisty ushering of romantic love, it must be the songs (affectionately called Rabindrasangeet) of Gurudev Tagore. It has been resilient to myriad experimentations, emerging as eternal as Music itself. Furthermore, Nazrulgeeti, Shyamasangeet, Dwijendrageeti, Atulprasadi and Prabhat sangeet have ensured that the ticking of the clock is never a threat that looms large enough on the aesthetic space of Bengali music. The smell of the earth, like memories unattended, saturates the air every time Bhatiyali, Bhawaiya, Dhamail, Gombhira or Baul is played within the earshot. That musicians in Bengal have been successful in fusing international influences with tradition to serve a delectable platter, is substantiated by the success of Bangla Rock—a force to be reckoned with, since its inception through Moheener Ghoraguli. The legacy has been perpetuated by Bhoomi, The Anupam Roy Band, Chandrabindoo and Cactus, to name a few.

The shared past of West Bengal and Bangladesh makes it scarcely feasible to compartmentalize Bengali music into these two brackets. Their shared present continues to weave a melodious future where music makes the native roots inescapable for a Bengali in any corner of the world.

ঋতুদা.. তোমার জন্য..

Priyanka Chatterjee

দিনটা ছিল ৩০ শে মে, ২০১৩... সেদিন অনেক বেলা অবধি ঘুমিয়েছিলাম। ঘুমটা ভাঙল পাশের ঘর থেকে আসা টিভি-র একটা খবর শুনে। জাতীয় ও আন্তর্জাতিক স্তরে খ্যাত বাঙালী পরিচালক ঋতুপর্ণ ঘোষের অকস্মাৎ মৃত্যু। মনে হল স্বপ্ন দেখছিলামতো! কিছুক্ষণেই বুঝলাম, নাহ্! এটাই সত্যি। টিভি-র কাছে গিয়ে দেখলাম তাঁর নিথর দেহ। বিভিন্ন ক্ষেত্রে বিখ্যাত শিল্পী এবং অন্যান্যরা বললেন- চলচ্চিত্র জগতের এ এক বিরাট নক্ষত্রপতন। আমার কাছে ঘটনাটা হয়ত কিছুটা অন্যরকম ছিল। তাঁর প্রতিটি ছবির মুক্তির আমার নিদারুণ অপেক্ষা সেদিন শেষ হয়েছিল। তিনি আর নতুন কোন ছবি পরিচালনা করবেননা এটা মানতে পারছিলামনা। তাঁর পরিচালনাকৃত আমার দেখা প্রথম ছবি "উনিশে এপ্রিল"। আমি তখন স্কুলে পড়ি। শুধুমাত্র দুটি চরিত্রের কথোপকথন দিয়ে এত অসাধারণ ছবি তৈরি করা সম্ভব তা আমি ভাবতে পারতামনা যদি না এই ছবিটি দেখতাম। স্বাভাবিকভাবেই আমার ছবি পছন্দ করার মান অনেকটা উচ্চতায় উঠে যায়। তারপর একে একে তাঁর আরো কিছু অসাধারণ ছবি দেখতে থাকি। শুধু তাঁর সৃষ্ট ছবি-ই নয়, তাঁর নির্ভীক ও স্পষ্টবাদী ব্যক্তিত্ব আমাকে আকর্ষণ করতে থাকে। তিনি তাঁর স্বতন্ত্রতার সঙ্গে কখনও আপোষ করেননি। তিনি আমাদের সমাজ-আরোপিত লিঙ্গের বিরোধিতাও তিনি তাঁর ছবির মাধ্যমে তুলে ধরেছেন। একজন জীবিত মানুষের সাথে দীর্ঘদিন

ধরে বিশ্বাসঘাতকতা করা এবং তাঁর মৃত্যুর পর তাঁর প্রতি বিশ্বস্ততা.. এমনই জটিল কাহিনীকে নিপুণভাবে তুলে ধরেন তিনি "সব চরিত্র কাল্পনিক" ছবিতে। "অন্তরমহল" ও "চোখের বালি" ছবিতে তিনি আমাদের সমাজের কিছু কুৎসিত দিক তুলে ধরেন, যেগুলো হয়তো আলোচনা করতেও অনেকে দ্বিধা বোধ করবেন। তাঁর এই প্রয়াস আমাকে সর্বদা অনুপ্রাণিত করে। একটা ইচ্ছে ছিল মনে তাঁকে সচক্ষে চিত্র পরিচালনা করতে দেখা, ওঁনার সাথে কিছু সময় কাটানো। কিন্তু এ বড়ই অলীক ইচ্ছে। আসলে আমাদের সব ইচ্ছেগুলো বাস্তববাদী হয়না। উনি আমাদের বাংলা চলচ্চিত্র জগতকে অন্য মাত্রায় পৌঁছে দিয়েছেন। উঁনি না থাকলেও, ওঁনার কাজের মধ্যে দিয়ে উঁনি সর্বদা আমাদের মনের খুব কাছাকাছি থাকবেন॥

A Literary Stroll Through Boi Para

Kasturi Patra

I LOVE BOOKS. In fact, I'm a bit obsessed about those seemingly ordinary flat objects made of paper, ink and glue, that like magic spells, have the power to transport readers to a different time and place, filling them with emotions they never knew existed. My love for books had been lovingly nurtured by Kolkata. Being brought up in a city, whose very fabric is intricately woven with the spirit of some of the finest literary figures infused within me the spirit of a voracious reader. Here, I will write about my love affair with College Street, fondly known as the boi para (loosely translated as the book colony).

I've recently learnt a word, vellichor, which means the nostalgia induced by used bookstores. Like a sepia tinted photograph, frayed at the edges with the passage of years, the word brought back images of my own boi para before my mind's eye. I feel the word was invented specially to describe

College Street, the world's largest second-hand book market and the largest book market in India. For me, happiness entails a leisurely afternoon in College Street, browsing through old and weathered books, the college buildings looming in the background like timeless protectors, the grey cloud-laden sky perfectly complementing the image. Like the Gingerbread House in the fairy tale that lured Hansel and Gretel, College Street entices bibliophiles of all ages with the promise of satisfying their literary cravings. You can spend hours browsing through books, pestering the booksellers with myriad questions, bringing down entire shelves to choose just a few out of the pile.

Boi para lovingly caters to those nostalgia stricken bibliophiles, who like to go through stacks of old books in makeshift stalls that are kept in no particular order except for their sizes to maintain the balance. Worn out spy thrillers to fity-year-old knitting books, old Russian magazines to American teen comic books. You will enjoy wading through the sea of this eclectic collection in order to reach the ones that you want to take back.

No description of College Street is complete without mentioning the popular eateries dotting the place from Paramount's Juice Corner serving Daab Sharbat to Putiram's kochuri, the cutlets at Basanta Cabin, to College Street's famous landmark, Coffee House. Standing in the shadow of its erstwhile glory, Coffee House might not serve the best food and beverages presently, but for the sake of old times, you'd still love to visit the premises that was once frequented by some of the greatest intelligentsia of Bengal.

College Street's charm for me lies in its lack of glamour. It is old and looks a bit tired in its unkempt appearance. It bears no resemblance to a typically young and urban hangout spot. And maybe that's why hopeless romantics and hardcore bibliophiles like me can't stop loving it even more. Because like a book that shouldn't be judged by its cover, it'll be wrong to judge this literary treasure trove by its outward appearance.

God's Own Abode

Rupsha Bhadra

WHEN YOU HEAR the word 'art' you probably think of, 'The Starry Night' by Van Gogh, the much debated 'Mona Lisa', Tagore or Jogen Chowdhury. Few would think of this quaint place called Kumortuli, full of narrow lanes, in North Calcutta, that according to me, hosts some of the world's most talented artists.

Well, that is where the Goddess comes to life. Ask me how? It's the place the idols are made for Durga Puja, a four-day-long festival that takes the state by storm in the month of October and witnesses brilliant lights, crowded streets, new clothes, song, dance and more.

I've had the privilege of visiting Kumortuli a couple of times with my father. Each time, I've left the place more fascinated than the previous time.

God making is a difficult task.

A basic structure is first made of bamboo tied with cords.

It is given anatomical shape by binding layers of straw on it. Clay, specially brought from the banks of the river Ganges, is applied on the straw giving the idol her body, curves and limbs. The faces are made separately in moulds and then attached to this structure. Then starts the painting. There are idols done up just in white and there are ones which are vibrant in different hues. The eyes, which sort of bring her to life, are drawn on Mahalaya, seven days before the festivities begin. She is then draped in colourful sarees and adorned with artificial jewellery.

Here's why I think it's a place that nourishes talent like no other.

The workers don't have fancy studios with great lighting, or large spaces to work in. They have tiny rooms, each of which houses over twenty idols cramped together. In spite of all of this, work is completed on time, shipped to foreign lands and the idols look as divine as always. The sizes of idols can be more than double of the person working on it, and he can barely look at it from a distance of four meters or lesser. And yet, the proportions remain perfect. There is hardly any light after dark, and yet they manage to paint and dress up Ma Durga and her four children in all their glory. There are rainy days, when almost no substantial work is possible and power cuts which spell doom.

It is a place that has a story in every nook and corner with artists having worked on this over generations. Work here starts over five to six months in advance with each artist having numerous deliveries to cater to and deadlines to meet.

People all over the world probably hear of the festivities, fun and madness that occur in the four days. Few know of what goes on in order to make that happen. Few know of the hardships these artists face.

So if you say 'art' to me, this is what I think of. The magic of Bengal, captured in a few narrow lanes, that can easily be called the home of the Goddess.

'Bengoal' Right Ahead

Arinjay Ghosh

THROUGH THE RELENTLESS pursuit of excellence, Bengal is taking giant strides in sports in general and the beautiful game in particular. Bengal has always been the 'home and hub of Indian football,' right from the halcyon days of Goshto Pal, Chuni Goswami and the likes. But in the early part of the new millennium, Goa had edged ahead in the domestic honour list and the tag of 'home and hub' was quietly smirked at; mainly because the traditional giants, Mohun Bagan and East Bengal were just mid-table pushovers. The hurt was evident and concerns kept growing.

But there goes a saying, 'What Bengal thinks today, India thinks tomorrow.' In 2014, a franchise team from Bengal won the inaugural edition of the Indian Super League with a local boy, Mohammad Rafique, scoring the winning goal in the final. As it turned out, that was a harbinger of things to come. The IFA, governing body of football in Bengal, built an academy called Pailan Arrows that scouted Under-19 players from every part of the state. This academy slowly morphed into a team which then participated in the I-League. The team had a sobering experience in 2013 because at that time Pritam Kotal, Narayan Das, Sehnaj Singh, Pronay Haldar, Bikash Jairu were greenhorns not used to the big time. Today, alongwith Anrab Mondal, Subrata Pal and Rahim Nabi, those same players form the backbone of the national football team. Sunil Chhetri, the India captain and all-time leading goal scorer, learnt his trade in Mohun Bagan, a club based in Bengal.

On the more advertized domestic front, Bengal has reclaimed the baton of football from Goa and is now far ahead of its counterparts. Mohun Bagan won the I-League last season and in this current season are fighting for national glory along with East Bengal, another torchbearer for Bengal football. Both teams are being coached by men from Bengal.

The IFA Shield, in its 120th year of existence, is the second oldest tournament in the world after the FA Cup. This speaks volumes about the commitment to professionalism Bengal has towards sports.

I have been working with the All India Football Federation recently as a reporter and I will use my first-hand experience to share with you a few facts about the inspiring ground reality. The India Under-17 team for the World Cup has ten players bred in Bengal including captain Amarjit

Singh. This team travelled to Spain and beat Elche Under-17 2-0 before hammering higher ranked Asian teams, Bahrain (5-0) and Lebanon (6-0), in the AFC Championship. In the last match played, they demolished Botswana (10-1). The immediate juniors playing for the AIFF Academy Under-19 team have seven players in their squad from Bengal. They have bested the Malaysian junior champions in their own backyard and have also beaten Crystal Palace Under-19.

Bengal, thus, isn't just the home to the second largest football stadium in the world, but is also the heartbeat of Indian football.

Yes 'Bengoal', proudly dribble ahead.

The Idiosyncratic Collectivity

Samuel Prateek Toppo

THE SKY MORPHS into brilliant shades of crimson and mauve, as the sun sets on another tired, humid Kolkata day. As the sky transitions into a darkness that even the stars cannot pervade, I marvel at the sights that this bustling metropolis has to offer. The street lamps are lit, casting vast orange halos of light onto the now dark and crowded streets, bursting with people eager to get home; tired, burdened, dripping with perspiration. Somewhere a street urchin cries out infinitely for alms.

This city is a beautiful city. She cradles children of all shapes and sizes and ideologies, sheltering them close to her heaving bosom; a bosom heaving under the load of two mass exoduses and a crumbling economy, kept alive and throbbing only by way of her children's unfounded hope for better days to come. It is this hope that sustains the wheels of humanity in motion. While the earth rotates for yet another day, this teeming collectivity of people from all walks of life systematically synthesises its existence into one comprehensive whole, abounding with various anomalies and dysfunctions, yet getting by all the same.

The playgrounds are now empty, and the children are home, some by candle light and some by electric lamps, building a future. My future had been built many decades ago, when buses ambled along their routes, didn't race and charged twenty-five paise as minimum fare.

On a good day, if your cellphone ran out of charge, or you forgot it at home, you would have noticed me. I carry a bag and an iron ring. In the latter contraption, I showcase my wares for you to eat, if you notice me. Day by day, it becomes increasingly difficult for someone like me to break even. Although I live alone, a man must amount to something, and provide for himself. Every day I see and experience the myriad pains and struggles and joys that my co-passengers choose to exhibit. To see a little child's face light up at the offering of my candies is an accomplishment. Or to see a young boy, under his schoolbag burden, seeking an iota of light from the dim lamps to read his favourite novel. Every day I take part in the collective joys and sufferings of the people in this city, this Mahanagar. Every day, I return to an empty abode on a lonely street, cramped by the vast enveloping darkness.

You would not believe it, but this city is generous. The

people are generous. Daily, the bus conductors help me with my load; sometimes they don't. I choose not to generalize. Ah, Uluberia is here. That's my stop. You see, I don't live in Kolkata. It is my adopted home, for a few hours, just as it is for many millions. I do not make much, just enough to get by. My reward is in the experiences I witness daily, on those bustling streets and crowded buses of that mad, idiosyncratic collectivity called Kolkata.

অনুরণন

Sudipta Nath

সময়ের সাথে সাথে আমাদের চারপাশের বদলটা মনের কোনো এক নোম্যানসল্যান্ডে ছাপ ফেলে। আধুনিক নাড়াচাড়ায় পুরাতনী আড়মোড়া ভাঙে কখনওবা।আর্বান বোরডম কাটাতে বাঙালী বৈশাখের পয়লায় ভজহরির ডাকবাংলো মটন আর নলেনের আইসক্রিম দিয়ে বাঙালিয়ানা পালন করে।তবুও মায়ের শাড়িতে লেগে থাকা হলুদের ছোপের মতন বাঙালির নিজস্ব কালচার ও দাগ রেখে যায় আমাদের প্রত্যেকের গভীরে। হয়তো তাই,গম্ভীর,ফ্যাশনদুরস্ত কর্পোরেট কন্যাটিও পঁচিশে বৈশাখে আনমনে গুনগুন করে ওঠে - "তুমি কেমন করে গান করো হে গুণী...." সরস্বতীপূজোয় আপনা থেকেই জিন্স/কুর্তায় অনীহা হয়।মায়ের আলমারি থেকে হাতছানি দেয় পাটকরা বাসন্তী ঢাকাই। লা মার্টসের যে ছেলেটি কথায় কথায় পাওলো কোয়েলহো আওড়ায়,নিবিড়ে বান্ধবীর দীঘল কালো চোখে চোখ রেখে গায়- "তা সে যতই কালো হোক,দেখেছি তার কালো হরিণ চোখ..." কাস্টার্ড,পুডিং খাওয়ার আনন্দ ছাপিয়ে যায়, যখন লক্ষী পূজোর পরে,অফিসে কলিগের লাঞ্চ বক্স থেকে বেরোয় নারকেল নাড়ু আর তিলের লাড্ডু। এরম আরো অনেক কিছু যা মনে করিয়ে দেয় যে মাটির ভিতরে শিকড়ের টানটা কতোটা মজবুত। আমাদের এই গতিশীল পথচলায়,কতো টুকরো টুকরো অভ্যাস রপ্ত করেছি আমরা।"ফাস্ট লিভিং"-এর দোহাই দিয়ে আমরা ব্যস্ত হয়েছি।সোশ্যাল নেটওয়ার্কিং এর হাজারো

বন্ধুর ভীড়ে পাড়ার বন্ধুর সাথে দূরত্ব বাড়িয়েছি।তবুও,ঠিক যেমন পুরোনো বইয়ের গন্ধ বুকভরে শুঁকে নেওয়ার সুখকে ছাপিয়ে জায়গা করে নিতে পারবে না ই-বুক,ঠিক তেমনই নতুনের ভীড়ে পুরনো হারাবার নয়। সময়, জীবনের ছোটবড় মেমেন্টো কুড়িয়ে নিজ ছন্দে বয়ে যাবে।নতুনের ছোঁয়াচ লেগে আমাদের মলাট টা যাবে বদলে,তবে ভেতরকার মানুষটা শিকড় ছুঁয়ে থাকবে ঠিক। এই যে হাত ছেড়ে গিয়েও ধরে থাকা,চোখের আড়ালে থেকেও ভীষণ ভাবে জুড়ে থাকার নামই সংস্কার। যা আলগোছে আমাদের কড়েআঙুল ছুঁইয়ে থাকে।আর হয়তো তাই,এই দ্রুত বদলে যাওয়া শহরের আকাশে যখন গোধূলির মায়াআলো লেগে থাকে,অনেকদূর থেকে ভেসে আসে,গেরস্তের শঙ্খধ্বনি,অজান্তেই আঙুল কপাল ছুঁইয়ে যায় শৈশবের অভ্যাসে, বাড়ির জন্য মনকেমন করে।ফ্ল্যাশব্যাকে ফিরে আসে তুলসীতলার মায়ের সন্ধ্যাপ্রনাম। প্রাত্যহিক ব্র্যান্ডেড পোশাকের অভ্যস্ততায়,মায়ের হাতেবোনা মাফলার,কার্ডিগান এক চিরন্তন স্টেটমেন্ট,যা ঘর থেকে বহুদূরে থাকা ছেলেটিকে লন্ডনের জুবুথুবু ঠান্ডাতেও স্মৃতিমেদুর ওম দিয়ে ভালোবেসে যায়। আমাদের সংস্কৃতি আমাদের মননে,আত্মায়। ছোটোবেলায় দাদুর দেওয়া আদুরে ডাকনামের মতো,যা মনের আনাচেকানাচে অনাবিল আনন্দ এনে দেয়,বিদেশ বিভুঁইয়ে পড়ে থাকা প্রবাসী ছেলেটিকে আরো একবার মনে করিয়ে দেয় তার ঘর,বাড়ি,তার ছেলেবেলার স্কুল,শৈশবের প্রেম,তার প্রথম সবকিছু । ক্ষয়িষ্ণু বিকেলের শেষ আলোয় তখন সে আনমনে গেয়ে ওঠে—"আমি বাংলায় গান গাই..আমি বাংলা কে ভালোবাসি...."

Creative Flourish in Bengal Cinema

Archita Mittra

EVER SINCE SATYAJIT Ray's *Pather Panchali* won acclaim at the 1956 Cannes Film Festival, Bengal cinema established itself as a creative industry capable of innovative and poignant storytelling, rivalling the likes of commercial Hollywood blockbusters as well as European arthouse films. Along with the craft of Mrinal Sen, Bimal Roy and Ritwik Ghatak, Bengal cinema proved itself to be distinctively different from Indian filmic practices, unafraid of experimentation or unconventional subject matter, blurring the line between the commercial and the aesthetic by producing state of art films on relatively low budgets that combine international influences with local cultural styles and folklore, that simultaneously influence the international screen as well.

The new generation of film makers have not only continued these trends but have also reversed and reinvented familiar tropes to create works of fresh aesthetic value. A prime example would be the films of LGBT rights activist, Rituparno Ghosh that are marked by a feminine sensitivity and eye for detail. *Raincoat*, a reimagination of an O. Henry tale, explores the familiar love story genre with simplicity, sincerity and an unanticipated twist in the ending. The devastatingly beautiful adaptation of Tagore's *Chokher Bali* is poetry on celluloid, and *The Last Lear* localizes Shakespeare for a Bengali audience. Meanwhile, Q's cult films *Gaandu* and *Tasher Desh* take experimentation to a whole new level with the latter detailing a prince's existential crisis and quest for freedom with a psychedelic *Alice in Wonderland* touch, a graphic novel narrative influence and a new perspective on Tagore's songs with feminist undertones. Similarly, debutante Aditya Vikram Sengupta's *Asha Jaoar Majhe* that eschews dialogue altogether is a love letter to the old world charm of North Calcutta that mixes magic realist elements to detail the breakdown of a domestic relationship.

In terms of innovative storytelling, Srijit Mukherji's thriller *Chotushkone* interweaves several tales within a single narrative, like a Russian doll within a doll toy—a definite signal of a post-modernist meta narrative strategy. Other film makers explore previously neglected subject matters, tapping into Bengal's rich cultural traditions and heritage. Notable examples include *Chotoder Chobi* (dealing with the lives of circus dwarves), *Nirbashito* (a biopic of exiled feminist writer Taslima Nasreen), *Moner Manush* (exploring the unique

Baul music and folklore traditions) and *Open Tee Bioscope* (a coming of age story, marked by a nostalgic flavour).

Finally, on the commercial front, we have the steady supply of detective movies, featuring household favourites like Feluda, Byomkesh and Kakababu as well as intelligent comedies such as *Bhooter Bhabishyat* and *Goynar Baksho* that also highlight the plight of Bengal's exquisite heritage buildings that deserve to be preserved and treasured. Meanwhile, Mainak Bhaumik is another interesting phenomenon. While *Maach Mishti And More* is the typical family comedy drama, *Aami Aar Amar Girlfriends* is Bengal's version of *Sex and the City* that celebrates the power of female bonding.

Thus Bengal cinema represents a unique cinematic practice that subverts genres and conventions to create films that are simultaneously critically acclaimed as well as commercially successful.

Citius Altius Fortius

Resham Das

WEST BENGAL HAS always produced some exceptional talents in the field of sports. The renowned sporting personalities, the feats they have achieved and the enthusiastic sports lovers from Bengal, all flourish as some of the most valuable assets of my state.

Kolkata-born British sprinter Norman Pritchard started the tradition of triumph in sports from Bengal, by winning two Olympic silver medals, representing India in athletics, back in 1900. Mihir Sen and Arati Saha were the first Indian man and woman to swim across the deadly English Channel, while Masudur Rahman Baidya was the first ever physically handicapped person to swim across the Strait of Gibraltar. Surya Shekhar Ganguly and Dibyendu Barua are renowned names in the field of chess from Bengal. Leander Paes, the legendary tennis doubles player is also a Kolkata boy. Football and cricket are the principal sports played in Bengal. Gostho

Pal, Krishanu Dey, P.K. Banerjee, Sailen Manna, Asiad Gold-winner Indian team skipper Chuni Goswami, are all big names of Indian football and they hail from Bengal. Mohun Bagan, East Bengal, Mohammedan Sporting, ISL Season 1 champion Atlético de Kolkata are some noted football clubs of India, having their bases in Kolkata. Bengal has won thirty-one Santosh Trophy national football tournaments, the most ever by any Indian state. Ex-cricketer, former Indian captain, present State Board President, and Atlético de Kolkata's owner, Sourav Ganguly is considered to be one of the best sportspersons from Bengal. Test wicketkeeper Wriddhiman Saha and Indian strike bowler Mohammed Shami and woman cricketer Jhulan Goswami are other big names from Bengal at present, while Pankaj Roy and Arun Lal were in the past. Kolkata Knight Riders, the IPL franchise from Bengal has won the IPL trophy twice!

Achievement in diverse sports is appreciated here. Saurav Ghoshal in squash, Mouma Das in TT, Anirban Lahiri in golf, Joydeep Karmakar in shooting, and Chhanda Gain in mountaineering made Bengal proud repeatedly.

Eden Gardens Cricket Stadium is known worldwide for housing the loudest and most cheerful gallery ever, which comes to life during all matches! Salt Lake Yubabharati Stadium is the highest-capacity football stadium in Asia, as it hosts an average 1,20,000 football lovers in a Kolkata Derby between Mohun Bagan and East Bengal. The Netaji

Indoor Stadium, Shiliguri and Durgapur Stadium, RCGC often hosts international tennis tournaments, kabaddi, TT, football matches and golf respectively.

Jagmohan Dalmiya, the former BCCI and ICC President, and the brain behind Asian unity in ICC, was from Kolkata. Mohammed Azharuddin, Sachin Tendulkar, Rahul Dravid, and many foreign cricketers often praised the enthusiasm of sports fans from Bengal. Many young sports aspirants are emerging out of the rural areas of Bengal, and that's an area in which my state has excelled. To fulfil the dream of achieving more Olympic medals, Bengal can provide handsome amount of athletes and sportspersons, who can work extremely hard to achieve the gold medal with the national anthem ringing in the backdrop.

West Bengal—It's Heart Over Head for the Residents

Aviroop Mookherjee

'IS THE EXIT straight ahead?' I had once asked an elderly gentleman at Kalighat Metro Station. 'Yes, where do you want to go?' he enquired.

'Chetla,' I replied. 'Where in Chetla?' he pressed further.

'Near the Chetla Bridge,' I retorted a bit impatiently.

Thereafter, the passerby proceeded to give me unasked-for details, like which auto should I take, fare details and exact travel time. He spent around three minutes of his time for me, when an affirmative nod would have sufficed. For those habituated to the breakneck pace of a Mumbai or Delhi, this affable Bengali Bhadrolok's actions may seem irritating or even intrusive, but it's this quintessential caring nature of the masses that makes West Bengal and its metropolitan capital different, and so endearing.

There are countless avenues where Bengal as a state could

get bragging rights over its counterparts.

Natural beauty (the only state which can boast of having snow-capped mountains as well as pristine beaches), a plethora of literary geniuses, stalwarts in music and sports, torchbearers of India's freedom movement and pioneers in science and thought leadership. Yet the charm of the state lies in the disarming humbleness of its people, the encapsulating feeling of bonding and brotherhood that it gives to even strangers. Unlike other metropolises, and even non-metropolitan cities like Pune, Bengaluru or Hyderabad, Kolkata moves at a leisurely pace. Here, people steadfastly refuse to sacrifice the small pleasures of life for materialistic gains. For office-goers, reaching on time is important, but only after having completed the satiating breakfast of hot radhaballavis (stuffed puris) with aloor dom (potato curry). Shopkeepers do not forsake their afternoon nap to earn a few extra bucks between 2 and 5 p.m., nor do compulsions of next day's urgent presentation desist working professionals from indulging in the evening adda (chit chat) on sports and politics. The rigors and hardships of everyday life do not inhibit these people from sparing a thought for others, from lending a helping hand to the needy. It's a city where an accident victim will be immediately rushed to the hospital by a group of complete strangers jostling amongst themselves to be the leader of the rescue mission; where a misdemeanour against a lady by a roadside Romeo on a crowded bus will result in a sound thrashing by fellow passengers; where ten unknown people will jump in to give road directions to a lost Hindi speaking newbie in a busy street, even if he asks one for guidance. It's another matter though that the atrocious Bengali-infused Hindi of the self-appointed guides will leave him more confused than earlier. Kolkata is that rare metropolis, where next door kakimas (aunts) prepare the most lip smacking mutton ghugni (yellow peas curry) to commemorate trivial events like you topping your Standard VII history exams.

Kolkata and Bengal will continue to awe by producing a steady stream of luminaries, but it's the intrinsic warmth of its residents that sets it apart in India and the rest of the world.

My Tryst with Bangaliana

Moyurie Som

BENGAL IS NOT just a state but a state of mind. A colour palette strewn with the red smear of our vibrant history, the hues of our art and culture and the marks left behind by those who make Bengal what it is today. Bengal is the magnificence of the northern mountains and the blue of the southern seas, it is the rivers that cascade down the lush meadows, it is the azure of the autumn sky. It is the debate of the morning walkers in a tea stall, it is in the adda of the college-goers in Coffee House. Bengal is the celebration of colours in spring, and the celebration of the Goddess in autumn.

Growing up eventually exposed me to the other facets of the diverse Bangali culture. Say for instance, cinema. Be it a commercial film like *Paglu* or a National award-winning film like *Nirbashito*, Bengalis ensure Tollywood remains a force to be reckoned with. Literature, too, is an inseparable part of the Bengali soul—*Thakumar Jhuli* and *Khirer Putul* leaving behind their eternal essence in our childhood. The words and tunes of Tagore resonate with our hearts through the agonies of adulthood. And the Bengali detectives in the form of Feluda and Byomkesh Bakshi shall challenge us to a game of intellect as they solve crime after crime. For those who embrace literature like their clandestine paramour, there is Srijato, Nabanita Dev Sen, Shirshendu Mukhopadhyay et al as their refuge. And for the music lovers, maestros ranging from the likes of Kishore Kumar and Manna Dey to today's Shreya Ghoshal and Lagnajita Chakraborti, and genres ranging from Rabindrasangeet, Nazrulgeeti and Atulprasadi to the styles of Kabir Suman, Anupam Roy and Fossils, cater to the music loving Bengali.

To me the most important aspect would be the food, not just for its gastronomical brilliance but for the sentiment that all Bengalis share with it, especially with their 'Maer haater ranna' (food cooked by ones mother). To the Bengali, it is a matter of immense pride, as if it's like a legacy of their family name or an exclusive cuisine characteristic of their household. The celebration of 'Maer haater ranna' would extend to the grand family feasts and even the occasional mangsho-bhaat on Sundays.

And last but not the least is the Bengalis enthusiasm in sports, especially in football and cricket. If one takes an evening stroll through the bylanes of any locality one would encounter a fervent group of boys immersed in their game of gully cricket or football.

No one can be quite done with Bengal and what it has to offer. It remains in us like a teardrop of a probashi Bangali (non-residential Bengali) when he Skypes with his mother from across the seven seas, and the delight of a little child when he hears the fascinating tales of Apu and Durga from his grandfather. It remains deep in our core like an inextinguishable flame, moulding us into the global citizens of tomorrow.

বাঙাল ঘটি জমজমাটি

Srijata Chatterjee

বাংলা নিয়ে কি লিখব এ নিয়ে কিছুদিন ধরে মাথায় অনেক কিছুই ঘুরপাক খাচ্ছিল। আজ হঠাৎই ফেসবুক অন করতেই দেখলাম কোনো এক রসিক লোক আমাদের প্রিয় ভানু বন্দোপাধ্যায়ের কিছু বাছা বাছা হাস্যকর সংলাপ পরপর সাজিয়ে একটা কমিক ভিডিও বানিয়েছে। সেই পাঁচ মিনিটের ভিডিও দেখে হাসতে হাসতে পেটে খিল ধরার জোগাড় হল। পুরোনো বাংলা সিনেমা দেখার অভিজ্ঞতা অনেক কম হলেও ভানুর মুখে "মাসিমা মালপো থামু" ডায়লগ শোনেনি এমন বাঙালি খুঁজে পাওয়া দায়। তবে রসটা শুধু ভানুর অভিনয়ে নয়, আমাদের প্রিয় বাঙাল ভাষার যাদুতেও অনেকটা বেশী রসময় হয়ে উঠত। বাংলা ভাষার এই মজার দিকটা হয়তো আমাদের অজানাই থেকে যেত যদি না প্রায় সাত দশক আগে পূর্ববঙ্গের (বর্তমান বাংলাদেশ) বাঙালীরা আমাদের বাংলায় এসে ঠাই নিত। এই সব ভাবতে ভাবতে হঠাৎ মনে হলো এইতো! পেয়েছি! পশ্চিমবঙ্গের বৈচিত্র্য তুলে ধরতে গিয়ে বাঙাল-ঘটি সম্পর্কে ফোকাস না করে কি থাকা যায়? তা এই বাঙাল কারা? আর এই ঘটি-ই বা কারা? ইতিহাসের কঠিন তথ্য পেশ করে এত সরল বিষয়টিকে জটিল করার কোন মানে খুঁজে পাচ্ছিনা। তাই পাতি বাংলায় বলতে গেলে যা দাঁড়ায় তা হল স্বাধীনতার পরে পরে যেসব বাঙালী পূর্ববঙ্গ ছেড়ে বাক্সপত্র নিয়ে পশ্চিমবঙ্গে চিরতরে চলে এল তারা হয়ে গেল বাঙাল আর যেসব বাঙালী

বরাবর এখানের-ই তারা হল ঘটি। আর তখন থেকে শুরু হল বাঙাল-ঘটির জমজমাট ভাব-আড়ির খেলা। থাবারের থালা থেকে ফুটবলের মাঠ পর্যন্ত ছেয়ে আছে বাঙাল ঘটির রেষারেষি। বাঙালদের লাল-হলুদের দিকে ঝোঁক থেকে শুরু করে পদ্মার ইলিশে টান সবেতেই যেন ঘটিদের টিপ্পনি কাটতেই হবে। আবার উল্টোদিকে সবুজ-মেরুন এর হয়ে পতাকা ওড়াতে ওড়াতে ঘটিদের প্রিয় গলদা চিংড়িকে জলের পোকা বলে এক কথায় নস্যাৎ করে দিতে না পারলে বাঙালদের পেটের ভাতই হজম হয়না! নেহাত চেহারার দিক থেকে কোনো অমিল নেই।কিন্তু তাতে কী? এ যেন উল্টো হব তাই উল্টে যাব ধরণের ইচ্ছে।এ বলে ঝাল তো ও বলে মিষ্টি; এ বলে আলু পোস্তো তো ও বলে মুড়ি ঘন্ট! তবে আমার মতো বাঙাল ঘটি মিক্সড প্রোডাক্ট দের হয়েছে ভারী সমস্যা।আমাদের আবার পৌষ পার্বণে থাবারের থালায় ঢাকাই পিঠের সাথে সাথে দুর্গাষ্টমীর সকালে অঞ্জলী সেরে থাবারের প্লেটে লুচি দুটোই চাই- ই চাই।একদিকে ঢাকাই জামদানী আর এক দিকে ফুলিয়ার তাঁত! এ বলে আমায় দেখ তো ও বলে আমায়। সিনেমা, গান, কবিতা, জোক্স হেন কোনো ফিল্ড নেই যাতে বাঙাল ঘটি দন্দ্ব ছাপ ফেলেনি। তবে কেউ কখনো এই লড়াই থামানোর চেষ্টা করেছিল কী? এই তথ্য আমার জানা নেই। তবে আমার বুদ্ধি তো বলে যদি আমায় কেউ এই লড়াই থামানোর কাজ দিত, আমিতো উল্টে ছোট্টো একটা টিপ্পনি কেটে ঝগড়াটা আরেকটু বাড়িয়ে দিয়ে চা আর সিঙাড়া খেতে খেতে রগড়টা দেখতেই পছন্দ করতাম। আর করব নাই বা কেন? এই বাঙাল ঘটির হাড্ডাহাড্ডি লড়াই থামেনি বলেই তো এপার বাংলা ও ওপার বাংলার সব ভালোটা মিলেমিশে একাকার হয়ে গেছে।আর তাছাড়া সবচেয়ে বড় কথা হল বাঙাল ঘটির মতো দুই সামাজিক দলের এমন কেমিস্ট্রি-র জুড়ি মেলা ভার! আপনি-ই বলুন সারা বিশ্বে এমন দন্দ্বের জুটি খুঁজে বের করা, ঘোড়ার ডিম খুঁজে বের করার চেয়ে কম কঠিন কাজ নাকি?

The Majestic Bong Mellows

Gurbinder Kaur

A LEGACY OF an incredibly magnificent and mighty cultural heritage she belongs to and the valour that's engraved in every anecdote of the past, she stood strong ever since with a spine of steel to witness the tangy humour genetically embedded, the vision of the opinionated who rarely shy away, the infectious charisma you just can't ignore. Besides, the myriad vibrant shades she offers, makes Bengal the beau idéal for the rest of the country. Having said that, I'm compelled to revisit the bygone childhood memories that have moulded me into a person I'm today. Rather she has been the guiding light for almost every time when things went topsy-turvy. My humble gratitude goes out to her undying spirit that didn't let me succumb to circumstances. An array of flashbacks is running through my mind yearning to be fabricated through expressions that could reach out. Those midnight cravings that don't settle for anything less than a rossogulla or the cozy blanket you ditch for the early morning walk at the Victoria Memorial, the streets rejoicing in utmost ecstasy during the Durga Pujo or the soothing calmness at Shantiniketan are a few instances of her multitudinous facets.

If you wish to experience all shades of art, sports, literature, culture and beyond, it has to be BENGAL. In our country, where traditions are taught even before the ABC's, Bengal is an exception. She has always viewed education as the breeding ground for intellectualism. Every ethnicity is known by its people who can hold onto their roots adapting with changes of the present. Bengal is seen to exhibit a judicious blend of vintage values and contemporary aspirations at the same time.

Here I take the opportunity to celebrate the joys of Bengal through poetry skills she has bestowed upon me over the years. Because for me, positivity lies in all those miniature incidents that you never thought could be so impactful. We should make an attempt to spread a good word, involve in noble deeds and show gratitude towards the native soil that has nurtured us into confident beings! Football is her first love, cricket her beloved child and music runs in her veins, art is her only respite. The kal boishakhi that sets summer on a spree, the majesty of the Sundarbans that's sheer beauty! The multicultural abode that welcomes everybody with open arms, don't take a sigh at the Lords (Politicians) Breakfree catacombs, resist all odds. Hopes never die when you're in Bengal, her children voice profound opinions. Tagore, Netaji, Amartya, Teresa are heroes of the past igniting quintessentials into modern day Chhanda Gayen, Shila Ghosh, Dhananjay Chakraborty and Prathna Sarkar. Days in and days out positive abstracts have been much talked about; lets turn them into fruitful actions, to leave behind us a more beautiful Bengal!

The Rise of a New Bengal

Madhutamo Sengupta

MY QUEST IN search of the 21st century Bengali spirit has driven me far and wide and taken me places where my soul felt a familiar, eternal connection to the flavour, to the essence, to the beauty of the language, to the palette of colours that blend perfectly to create the cradle of nature that fosters a tinge of adaptive modernisation with an everlasting respect for the past. I discovered evolution of a more refined modernized Bengali, yet his inner core radiates the same traditional fragrance prevalent since the birth of Bengal.

The new age Bengali is a unique blend of layers of emotions, values, love, respect, that has held on to the hunger for knowledge and enlightenment, the taste for tradition, the ear for good music; the exuberance of creativity each adding a different individual perspective to brew the new Bengal society. The current crop of Bengal is harvesting changes that wither the negativities of prejudices. No longer does gender, religion, caste limit them. Revolution of creativity, literature, science and technology lead the way, soaked in the sugary sweetness of the teachings of the founders of the Bengal society. The modern Bengali society has adapted the popular culture of the world without losing herself to it. Traditional contemporary Bengali folk has found its feet again with the likes of Suman, Anjan and Anupam bringing it to the world platter. Fusion of rock and jazz to both Rabindrasangeet and Baul has lifted many unknown compositions sung by the lips of the fishermen, saints, fakirs, or the locals to the world stage. Bengali bands are capturing the hearts of millions, yet the golden era of great musicians like Manna Dey, Hemanta, Dhananjoy, Sandhya and Arati are still popular.

The reincarnation of the Bengal cinema mediated through better story weaving clad in intellectuality finds its place equal to entertainers. The success of Anjan's Byomkesh or Sandip's Feluda tells us the new is walking hand in hand to the nostalgic times of Satyajit Ray, Mrinal Sen, Uttam Kumar, Soumitra. A new generation of directors and actors are providing a fresh outlook to Bengal cinema with unconventional, layered and unique subjects, even period drama like *Rajkahini* celebrates womanhood in a new light. Srijit Mukherjee, Aparna Sen, Abir, Saswata, Parambrata, are a few to name. Bengal still wakes up to the sounds of young voices practicing with the traditional harmonium and to the friendly banter over a cup of tea on topics that concern shaping the future with science and technology. An era of both industrial and educative development has coloured the face of Bengal with the paint of prosperity. Amidst all the change, one standout quality that has remained across the generations of Bengal is an affinity towards the roots, and the modern Bengali is progressing to a day where the mind is without fear.

The Complete Package: West Bengal

Rajni Shukla

SUCH WAS THE power of Rabindranath Tagore's pen that till today India chants 'Jana gana mana' as the National Anthem with pride. There was a time when we burnt women alive as sati in a barbaric fashion. It was Raja Rammohan Roy, the 'Father of the Indian Renaissance' who put enormous effort to establish the abolishment of this practice. If you are feeling low, come and read the books of Swami Vivekananda and get inspired. Today when the whole country is deriving entertainment from movies and daily soaps, then how can one forget Satyajit Ray, the greatest filmmaker, and his contributions? Football is the soul of Bengali people. But it is not that they are not interested in other games. Just initiate talks about Sourav Ganguly on the streets or local trains and let people join you uninvited. After all, the Prince of Kolkata is one of the greatest captains of the Indian cricket team whose captaincy changed the future of Indian cricket. If you want to see the passion for games, go to Eden Gardens (during cricket matches) or Salt Lake stadium (during football matches) and you will know what sports means for the people of Bengal.

Howrah Bridge, Victoria Memorial, Belurmath, Indian Museum, Sundarbans, Darjeeling Himalayan Railway and Tiger Hills, are just few of those amazing places that add value and beauty to West Bengal. Hand-pulled rickshaws and trams are still present in Kolkata to take you back in time.

If you are in search of land of festivals, come to Bengal and your search would be over. Durga Puja, Saraswati Puja, Kali Puja, Eid, Christmas day, Bengali New Year, Rath Puja, Mahalaya, Ram Navami, Rakshabandhan, Muharram and (the list goes on) are the festivals that West Bengal celebrates with great devotion and faith. Each festival brings with it lots of joy for its people and visitors.

Durga Puja, the most famous festival is celebrated with lot of enthusiasm throughout West Bengal. These festivals are the time when one can feel the culture, the traditions, the music and indescribable art that is the mark of excellence of West Bengal.

And if one is in Bengal, how can one control the appetite for rosogolla, maacher kalia, pulao and maach-bhaat. The soil had, has and will have plenty of talent by the grace of

God. From greatest actors to directors, singers to painters, writers to musicians, doctors to engineers, scientists and, of course, politicians can be traced from Bengal. The one who has seen the life of West Bengal prays to be born in this pious soil again and again. Because this place has all that any living person would ever want to have. And one life is not enough.

Tumi Ashbe Boley Taai

Nandini Nag

THE WESTERN WINDS blew the damp hair off her moist face as she sat languidly on her balcony, listening to the ululating sounds coming from the mandir, just next to her house. She never tired of listening to this 'ulu', even if it reminded her of the day she was leaving her Baba for her Bor, her in-laws. But that was another time, and another place.

Ma was getting ready along with Parijat, her little daughter, to go to the nearby puja pandal. They would be offering onjoli as it was Maha Navami, Durga Puja. Her saree lay folded on the bed, but she was not enthusiastic to go down. They would look at her again, chewing paan and say, with their tongues clucking, 'Aha go, her husband…it's so sad! How will she bring up her daughter?' But amidst all such concerns, she felt the onrush of adrenaline through her veins when she heard the dhak being played, the mahalaya agomoni song being played and numerous odours of food wafting through the air. She would be lying to herself if she pretended that she didn't miss her husband, the smell in his towel; and the empty space beside her on the bed gave her cramps every night. But some things are best left on their own and she would read Robithakur, who had shaped her thoughts and her existence since the time she was a little girl eating jhaalmuri. Only his writings saw her through all her ordeals, the little pleasures of life as described by him and the pain spoken of with such vividity. She would sing to her husband often, with his head on her lap... 'Amaro poraano jaha chaay...tumi taai' And they would float together on their love boat.

Today, she was alone, with him gone, but she forever preferred her own company, listening to *Thakumar Jhuli*, watching *Dadagiri*, or a match between Mohun Bagan and East Bengal, tuning into Sangeet Bangla, or even watching Pujo Porikroma on the local Bengali news channels, following the pujor adda among the Tollywood stars on TV. But the fact is would Kolkata ever make her feel that void in his absence? Where was the void? She would go and toss food to the fishes in the Lake and she could see him sitting on a bench on the other side, she would take a stroll around Esplanade and he would be there, haggling with a shopkeeper, she would see him in Banccharam, quickly gulping down hot rosogollas. He was there moulded into the soil of Kumortuli, he was there in smell of doi maach being cooked. And he would be there always, as eternal as the shadow of Howrah Bridge on the Ganga even if people repeatedly said 'Kolikata choliaachey, noritey noritey'. And she, Tilottama, would sit on the banks of Ganga to see him emerge from the golden waters, just like Kolkata.

আনন্দ ধারা

Sahel Ghosh

'আনন্দ ধারা' শব্দ তার মধ্যেই একটা অন্য রকম বাগান আছে। যেন বৃষ্টি ভেজা কলকাতার হৃদয় বিদীর্ণ করে বেরিয়ে আসা গান এর আহুতি। গ্রামবাংলার আন্দরমহল থেকে উঠে আসা জীবনের হাসি কান্না সমন্বিত এক নিবিড় ভালবাসার ছোঁয়া এই গান। সে কখনও রবীন্দ্রনাথের পদাবলি, কখন বা কীর্তন কখন ভাটিয়ালি কখনও বা বৈষ্ণব পদাবলি। এ ছাড়াও রয়েছে বাংলার নিজের কবিগান, কখন গম্ভীরা গান। লোক সমাজের গুঁতোয় নয়, এই গান এসেছে বাংলার মাটির টানে। মন খারাপ, আনন্দ, হাসি-কান্না সবটা জুড়ে আছে গান। একদিন এই গানই জুগিয়েছে স্বাধীনতার অনুপ্রেরণা। 'মা এর দেওয়া মতা কাপড়' মাথায় তুলে ক্ষুদিরামরা হাসতে হাসতে প্রান দিয়েছে। কখনও প্রেম করতে শিখিয়েছে 'গানের ওপারে' দাঁড়িয়ে থেকে। কখনও বিরহের যন্ত্রণা ভুলতে গেয়ে উঠেছি 'অশ্রু নদীর সুদূর পাড়ে হাট দেখা যায়, তোমার দ্বারে"। কীর্তন-এর টানে কখনও গেয়েছি "শ্রী কৃষ্ণ চৈতন্য, প্রভু নিত্যানন্দ", আবার ভাটিয়ালি টানে মাঝির সাথে কাঁধে কাঁধ মিলিয়ে গেয়েছি জীবনের গান। "মাঝ দইরা দিয়া" পাল তোলা নৌকা ছুট দিয়েছে। কখনও মালদাবাসীর রূপে দাদু (শিব)-কে নালিশ জানিয়েছি, খিস্তি অ দিয়েছি "গম্ভীরা"র রূপে। পুরাতন এর সাথে তালে তাল মিলিয়ে চলেছে নতুন ও। পঞ্চম থেকে শুরু করে কিশোর আশা লতা সন্ধ্যা ভেদ করে মান্না দে এর "coffee house"

এ বসে আড্ডা মেরেছি। হেমন্তের বাতাস গায়ে মেখে গেয়েছি "এই রাত তোমার আমার, এই চাঁদ তোমার আমার, শুধু দুজনের"। বাদ যাননি সলীল চৌধুরি ও। সন্ধ্যের আসরে শশিকান্ত কাহারবার বদলে দাদরা বাজিয়ে আসর ও মাটি করতে ছাড়েননি। 'হাজার টাকার ঝারবাতি'র তলায় মান্না মুগ্ধ হয়ে গান শুনেছি। শিং না থাকলেও তাকে সিংহ বলে তাও জেনেছি। তারপর কালের ধারা বেয়ে পৌঁছে গাছি একবিংশ শতাব্দীতে। 'একলা ঘর' থেকে বেরিয়ে আসার জন্য রুপম ইসলাম 'দেয় ডাক'। জিত গাঙ্গুলি বাংলার মাটিতে নতুন করে প্রেমের জোয়ার এনেছেন। শিলাজিতের গয়নে খুজেছি 'জলফড়িং' কে। 'বসন্ত' এর অকাল আগমনে মন খারাপ এর ঘরের কনে আনুপম বলেছে 'আমাকে আমার মত থাকতে দাও'। দুহাত দিয়ে ঝিনুক কুরিয়ে আঞ্জন দা কে বলেছি 'রঞ্জনা আমি আর আসবনা'। তবু গানওলা থেমে জেতে দেয়নি। গানওলার আদরেও ফুটে উঠেছে কান্না। তবু শুভমিতার সাথে বৃষ্টি পায়ে পায়ে হেঁটেছি। রুপাঙ্করের গান বেয়ে ভালবাসার গভিরে প্রবেশ করেছি। বঙ্গে কাঁপিয়ে ভারত নাচিয়ে বাবুল ফিরেছে নিজের বাংলায়। বাংলার গন্ডি পেরিয়ে বাঙ্গালিরা নাচিয়েছে ভারত কে। কুমার শানু, শান, শ্রেয়ারা স্বমহিমায় প্রজ্বলিত হয়েছে। প্রীতম চক্রবর্তীর সাথে 'আল্বিদা' যেমন বলেছি তেমনই শান্তানু মৈত্রর সিখে বলেছি 'কাহা গ্যায়া উসে ঢুন্ডো'। যুগ যুগ ধরে ভারত কে গয়নে গন্ধে ভরিয়ে তুলেছে বাঙালিরা। বাংলার গানের টানে দেশ-বিদেশ থেকে ছুটে এসেছে বহু মানুষ। বাংলা কে ভালোবেসে বাংলাই হয়েছে তাদের আস্তানা। অ্যান্টনি ফিরিঙ্গির কথা এর প্রমান সুচিত করে। এছাড়া এসেছেন আল্লা ইয়াম্নিক, ঊষা উথুপ, আশা ভোসলে, লতা মাঙ্গেস্কর এর মত কাল জয়ী শিল্পিরাও। এক কথায় যুগ যুগ ধরে বাংলা সমগ্র বিশ্বকে সমৃদ্ধ করেছে গানে গল্পে। ষড়জ থেকে নিষাধ অবধি বাঙ্গালিদের নিরলস পরিশ্রম অনস্বীকার্য। এটাই একজন বাঙ্গালির অহংকার। শেষ করার আগে বাংলার ফাটাকেষ্টর সুরে বুক চাপড়ে বলি "আমি বাঙালি, আমি গরবিত আমি বাঙালি"। ধন্যবাদ।

Parts of a Whole

Suchisubhra Sarkar

THERE'S NOTHING SPECIAL about Chakraberia Lane, where I've been raised. So the directions I give to Ola drivers didn't really catch my attention till the debate about intolerance started raging. 'Crossing the Jain temple, Terapanth Bhavan, take the right towards the monastery and drive straight till the green masjid. Ahead of it, take the right and stop in front of the Kali mandir.' The strangest part was that the driver didn't recognize the absurdity and near impossibility of having such diverse religious institutions peacefully coexisting along one road in these days of differences and outrage. Which is when I, chronic intern, traveller and debater in cities everywhere, realized that unlike in those places, Chakraberia Lane isn't an anomaly in the grand scheme of Kolkata—it's the norm.

As one of the first principles in debating, you're taught that communities are either individualistic (the audience responds with USA) or collectivist (Japan, the audience roars). The first tells you to have your own identity, live your own life and find freedom in cutting off ties that might hold you back. The latter makes you conform, become one among many and know that in homogeneity lies strength, because the community has your back. Here's where Kolkata, my Calcutta, becomes unfathomably beautiful. My city lets you be who you want to be—lovers of pork vindaloo don't stop you from cherishing Oly Pub's beef steak.

You could be a jhola-carrying Leftist by day and guitar-wielding biker at night. Here's a city of people who won't agree with you, often don't understand new-age ways and titter in disapproval. But here are the people who'll be the first to have your back; a city that might not empathize with homosexuals, but take to the streets to secure a voice for them. A city of students who join hands for a cause in Jadavpur that honestly doesn't affect their Park Street campus. Here's a city where you can embrace any religion, race, gender, profession, love Bollywood, have a personality that's uniquely yours, be an individual in the truest sense—yet be rest assured that the collective cares enough to fight for you when you need them.

Kolkata is a city that ensures students in a college, such as mine, coming from every corner of India, retain their individual identities without being alienated. It lets them celebrate these identities, even when they stick out awkwardly in white and gold sarees across the city on Onam—a festival Kolkattans hardly know about. However, this is the same city whose people stood by us and cared about us when we lost a friend. You could be in a Bangalore with its cosmopolitan identity, but you wouldn't be individuals who make up a caring collective the way Kolkata does. Rajesh Kaku next door disapproves of me taking Olas like that one late at night. But he's also the person who, when he notices me getting into one, unfailingly asks my father next morning if I reached my destination safely. That's Kolkata for you.

Flavours of Festivity in Bengal

Sourina Bose

THERE'S A SAYING in Bengali 'Bangalir Baro Mashe Tero Parban' and just to let everyone know, there's no doubt about it. For a quintessential Bengali, 'pujoparban' is the best way to portray the 'Bangaliana' culture. According to the 'panjika' (Hindu astronomical almanac), the Hindus have a twelve-month calendar. In the first month Baisakh (April–May), Bengalis celebrate 'poila boisakh' or Bengali New Year. It generally commences on the 14th or 15th of April every year. Not just new clothes and sweets, it also marks the commencement of new halkhata (financial record book) for businessman. Next up is Akshaya Tritiya, which is celebrated by worshiping Ganesha and Lakshmi.

Next is Jaishto (May–June). A social custom of a Bengali household during this month is 'Jamai Sashti'. 'Jamai' or the the son-in-law is treated with his favourite delicacies apart from being showered with gifts and goodies.

The monsoon ushers in 'Ashardh' (June–July) and Shrabon (July–August) with the celebrations of Rath Yatra where Lord Jagannath, his brother Balabhadra and their sister Subhadra travel in a Rath (chariot) to their aunt's place. To waive off troubles, Bengali women worship Bipodtarini, a goddess believed to be one of 108 avatars of Durga. Next in line is the popular occasion of Jhulan Yatra celebrated to mark the romance of Lord Krishna and Radha.

Bhadra (August and September) is the month when Bengalis host the worshiping of Lord Vishwakarma, the deity of all craftsmen architects. And then the Mother of all Bengali festival arrives—Durga Puja—in the month of Ashwin (September and October). Statistics say almost hundred crores are pumped into Bengal market during this time. After Goddess Durga returns to Kailash (her abode in heaven), Goddess Lakshmi (Kojagori Lakshmi Puja) arrives in Bengali homes for wealth and fortune. Shyama or Kali Puja is a festival dedicated to Goddess Kali celebrated on the new moon day of Kartik month (October–November). After Kali Puja, the brother–sister bonding gets a religious touch with the celebration of Bhatri Dwitiya. Agrahayan (November–December) is the ninth month where women perform Itu Puja. This puja is believed to increase prosperity of the husband and family members, while for the unmarried ones they do it in anticipation of having the best man.

In Poush (December and January) Makar Sankranti, a

festival generally held on the last day of this month to mark the harvesting, is celebrated. Bengalis gorge on pithe-puli' during this time.

Shukla Panchami of Magh (January and February) is destined for Saraswati Puja, the goddess of learning. Falgun (February–March) is colourful because of Doljatra and Basanti Puja. Chaitra (March–April) is the last month of the Hindu calendar with occasions like Neel Puja. It is performed by every mother for the well-being of their child, while Gajan is about remembering Lord Shiva. This culturally strong community and the state of Bengal does not just worship, they celebrate every bit of its culture in grandeur.

The City of Joy Speaks

Garima Behal

SHUPROBHAT, DEAR VISITOR! **Kemon acchen?** How are you doing, this morning? I notice it is your very first visit to me, the City of Joy. It has been two days since you disembarked at the railway station, all alone, with just one rucksack, on a shoestring budget! Tell me, did you find what you were looking for? Yesterday, I saw you charting out your journey, planning a long, solitary morning walk at the Howrah Bridge. And it pleased me to witness your exhilaration as you traversed the 700 metres with a spring in your step. You waited for the sun to rise across the river Hooghly and sat down on the banks, watching the water reflect the golden crimson hues of happiness. You breathed in deeply and watched the gurgling waters as the first ferries were unanchored from the shores. A ferry ride was not on your itinerary, but you went ahead, revelling in the slow bobble of the wooden boat on the waves. I watched your face break into a smile as the ferry rocked to the melody of Tagore's 'Ekla Chalo Re'. The lyrics mirrored your state of mind, your solo journey, the bliss you were seeking in solitude. Pardon me for following you around, but it makes me happy when I am able to make my visitors joyous, staying true to my name. Oh, and I never knew you were staying with a true blue, hospitable Bengali family. I realized it only when you wandered back, hungry from the morning excursion. You were a little sceptical about the meals in Kolkata, but the first bite of the ghugni made you change your mind. I assure you no one minded when you took two extra helpings! The lady of the house would have been delighted by your implicit praise, because she promised you fresh macher jhol for lunch, right?

You dressed up traditionally, in a lungi and took pictures with them. Your grinning faces will stay imprinted in my memory. You stepped out again in the evening, and were awed by the trams. Perhaps you didn't know I am the only Indian city with a functional network of trams, and the oldest in Asia to have so? Boy, that makes me proud! You experienced a comfy ride to Victoria Memorial and your mind raced like the tram, taking in the music, the chatter of a foreign but mellifluous tongue, the sharp tang from the phuchka stalls and the riot of colours on the autumnal streets.

Impressed by the architectural wonder of the Memorial, you made your way to Park Street and window shopped.

You came back tired but renewed and I wish I could see myself through your eyes. Because, today, I know you have fallen in love with me! And, today, I want to let you know that I love you, too! You will leave one day, but I promise, my memory will never leave you!

Life in a Metro

Advika Jalan

I'M A COLLEGE student. Needless to say, I'm usually short of both time and money. The Kolkata Metro is a saviour here— I'm rarely late for college, and I have to spend no more than ₹20 per day to travel from home to college and back. Since there are trains at every six-minute intervals, I never have to worry about missing one and being late. But that's not why I love the Metro. My parents are overprotective, and constantly call me up to check on me when I'm travelling. But they are comfortable with the idea of me travelling alone if I am going by the Metro because it is so safe. Metro gives me that sense of independence and confidence, and makes me feel like the 21st century woman I am. The other reason why I love the Metro is because of what I associate with it. The word for it is 'sonder,' which means 'the realization that each random passerby is living a life as vivid and complex as your own.' In the Metro, I see young working professionals heading to their workplaces. I see schoolgirls with braided hair and polished shoes. I see foreigners wearing Indian clothes, seeking the quintessential Kolkata experience. I see mothers dropping off their toddlers to preschool, and elderly ladies going to the market. In reality, my journey is only ten minutes long, but I can vicariously experience entire lifetimes in it. What makes the Metro so beautiful is that everyone, from all walks of life and all ages, use it. I fancy myself a keen observer of people, and what is a better place for it than the Kolkata Metro?

Kolkata is a diverse city, and the crowd I see in the Metro is an accurate representation of that diversity. There are several curious, amusing and heart-warming things about the Metro. For instance, the unwritten rule that eight women should sit on one bench (regardless of their girth). I often see corpulent women squeezing themselves into narrow spaces, and impressively enough, accomplishing that feat. Matronly women giving unsolicited advice to younger women. Young ones jumping to their feet and offering their seats to the elderly ladies and to the woman in the later stages of her pregnancy. Kolkata is characterised by warmth and concern for fellow travellers, and this is manifested in the interactions between the people travelling in the Metro. The idiosyncrasies and warmth of the people is rather charming. In fact, that's what gives the Kolkata Metro a soul, which I feel is conspicuously lacking elsewhere (perhaps I am being biased here).

Like Steve Maraboli said, 'It's funny how, in this journey of life, even though we may begin at different times and places, our paths cross with others so that we may share our love, compassion, observations and hope.'

The Kolkata Metro is not just a means of helping me reach my destination—it is a meaningful journey in itself.

"আমি আমার আমিকে চিরদিনই এই বাংলায় খুঁজে পাই...."

Srija Gupta

বাংলার সবুজ শ্যামল সরস প্রকৃতির জন্যই বাঙালি জন্ম-রোম্যান্টিক। এখানে একটি প্রচলিত কথা আছে বাংলায় এমন কোনো মানুষ পাওয়া যাবে না যারা জীবনে অন্তত একবারও কবিতা লেখেননি আর প্রতিটি বাঙালি বাড়িতে একটি 'সঞ্চয়িতা' বা 'গীতবিতান' এবং একটি ব্যবহৃত বা প্রায় ভুলতে বসা জন্মবৃত্তান্ত নিয়ে বিরাজ করা কয়েক দশক অব্যবহৃত হারমোনিয়াম থাকতে বাধ্য। দুর্গাৎসব প্রধান হলেও বাঙালির 'জীবনের উৎসব' পালিত হয় ২৫শে বৈশাখে,দোলে এবং অবশ্যই সরস্বতী পুজোয়। বাংলার মানুষ উৎসবে মাতে না,তারা আত্মিকভাবে উৎসবে মিশে যায়। চেনা অচেনার বেড়া ডিঙিয়ে তারা মাখিয়ে দিতে পারে ভালোবাসার ফাগ। বাঙালি আনন্দের সময় বলে উঠতে পারে "পাগল আমার মন জেগে ওঠে" আর মনখারাপের ধূসর বিকেলে কোনো বাঙালি কন্যা আনমনে বসে থাকে "শেষের কবিতা" হাতে ধরে এবং কোনো বাঙালি যুবক উদাত্ত কন্ঠে আবৃত্তি করে "কেউ কথা রাখেনি"। বাংলার মানুষের এই চির-রোম্যান্টিক সত্তাটি আমার বড় প্রিয়। তার জন্য সুশিক্ষিত হতে হয় না আমাদের। ট্রেনে,বাসে,রাস্তায় ফল,সবজি বিক্রেতারাও অদ্ভুত রসিক হন। এই রসবোধের পরিচয় পাওয়া যায়

বাংলার প্রাচীন সাহিত্য "চর্যাপদ" থেকে বিভিন্ন মঙ্গলকাব্যে। পরবর্তীকালে বিভিন্ন সাহিত্যিক থেকে শুরু করে রাজনীতিকদের মধ্যেও। বাঙালির চারিত্রিক দৃঢ়তার সঙ্গে স্বভাবরসিক সত্তাটি অদ্ভুতভাবে মিশে গেছে। যেমনভাবে বাংলায় উত্তরে হিমালয়ের গাম্ভীর্যের সাথে একসঙ্গে থাকে দামোদর,অজয়ের চঞ্চলতা আর শাল পলাশের রোম্যান্টিক সৌন্দর্য। বাংলার সন্তানরা সহজ মাটির সুরে জীবনের চরম সত্য বলতে পারেন,একতারার সুরে ভাবাতে পারেন বিশ্বকে। বাংলার বাউল,ভাটিয়ালীর সুরকে বাতাস ভাসিয়ে দেয় গ্রাম থেকে শহরে,শহর থেকে পুরো বিশ্বে। ছৌ নাচের তালে দুলে ওঠে তামাম দুনিয়ার মানুষের মন। আমার বাংলার প্রকৃতি যেমন বৈচিত্র্যময়,সরস,সুন্দর তার সন্তানরাও তেমনি। না,আমাদের নিজস্বসত্তাকে পারেনি গ্রাস করতে বিশ্বায়ন। আমাদের সংস্কৃতিকে,আমাদের সংস্কারকে আমরা বুকে আগলে রাখি পৃথিবীর যেকোনো প্রান্তে বাস করা সত্ত্বেও। মায়ের ভালোবাসার উপহার সেই সত্তা,যা চিরকালীন হয়ে রয়ে যাবে প্রজন্ম থেকে প্রজন্মে।

Filming Bengal

Aritra Basu

IN THE YEAR 1992, the greatest award for filmmaking was bestowed upon a stalwart filmmaker of all times—Satyajit Ray: a Bengali. Whereas it is beyond a shred of doubt that films like *Hirak Rajar Deshe* and *Pather Panchali* would remain in the list of films ever made, it should also be remembered that the place where these films were shot was in Bengal. Lush green fields through which Apu ran belonged to the land on which Ray was born: the land of Bengal. The music of the latter, composed in Bengal and smelling of it, gave it an indigenous sense of completion. Ray's compatriots like Mrinal Sen and Ritwik Ghatak also etched a mark in the film industry by producing pieces like *Kolkata Ekattor* and *Meghe Dhaka Tara* respectively, among other films. Sen was the first Bengali to introduce handle camera in Tollywood for which he received eternal fame, while the eclectic Ghatak created pieces which are taught in film schools nowadays.

After the end of the golden era in Bengali film industry, the sail was steadied by Rituporno Ghosh and Aparna Sen. Rituporno's *Chokher Bali* or Aparna's *Unishe April* will forever remain green in the memories of everyone in whose vein flows Bengali blood. Following the footsteps of Ray, Sen and Ghosh, filmmakers like Srijit Mujkherjee and Kaushik Ganguly used the modern day scenario to produce pieces of utter beauty like *Chotushkone* and *Sobdho*, respectively. The techniques used by these men of genius have overwhelmed critics and viewers all across the country, grabbing National Awards every now and then.

Being a Bengali fills one heart with pride to share the same piece of land and the same vernacular with these men of calibre. Bengali films have also seen veteran actors like Soumitra Chatterjee, who received the Dadasaheb Phalke award in 2012. These events, films, awards and the kindred things of awe and amazement bear testimony to the fact that Bengal is a place where films can prosper and flourish to their fullest. The general opinion of the people about cinema has also undergone severe changes over the past few years. Appreciation for quality movie-making has now become an inherent part of every Bengali who has got some education up his sleeve. Audiences from all across the state and beyond nowadays crowd the cinema halls to behold films like *Bela Sheshe* and *Open Tee Bioscope*.

Bengalis now know that films like *Khaad* and *Meghe Dhaka Tara* (directed by Kamaleswar Mukherjee) are worth their time. On a national scale, thus, Bengali cinema is making its mark, though late. Better late than never, though.

'She'

Deepsikha Chowdhury

WHAT IS 'BENGAL' for you? The cute white rosogolla or the tram? Most probably the gorgeous Victoria Memorial or the elevated Howrah Bridge. If not, then the arduous Durga Puja. But 'Bengal' from her perspective is a little dissimilar from that of ours. For her, rosogolla symbolizes a noteworthy occasion, the tram ride is an origin of euphoria. The grounds of Victoria Memorial is a mishmash of several unrequited love stories. The Howrah Bridge is a source of 'muse'. The joyous Durga Puja are 'days of high spirit' and Bengalis are the ideal people for gossip on every possible topic. She is the petrichor after the gushing monsoon rains, the paper boats in the water-logged streets that choke the drains. She is the peace after the 'kal-baisakhij'. She is the mishti-doi after a savouring lunch. The appetising great food that we munch. She is the 3 a.m. who knows all the disguised stories of the outcaste soul, the broken glass window that gives a bird's-eye view of the 'city of joy'. She is the passion for life; an epitome of 'bhalobasha'.

Kolkata's Affection Towards Durga Ma

Sreoshi Bakshi

AT THE CRACK of dawn, when the side streets of north Kolkata bore an evidence of emptiness and only a few rickshaw pullers had just begun waking up from their tiring night's sleep, Raghunath had already got into his frayed clothes and was applying his artistic skill on the face of the Durga idol at Kumartuli. His hands were crude and his clothes were shabby, giving away his poverty-stricken condition, but his eyes mirrored his self confidence and determination towards his job.

Durga Puja comes once in a year, but for him, every day is a chance meeting with Durga Ma, where he could nurture her, beautify her and embellish her in his own way. He prided himself in being the designer of the creator of the world. Raghunath may have deprivation in his life, but his commitment towards his artwork balanced out his pain and disappointment.

Indeed, it is true that Durga Puja comes once in a year but, we the people of Kolkata look forward to the magnificent five-day event eagerly throughout the year. Don't we all love the pujo-pujo feeling, when a luscious fragrance hovering above the Kolkata atmosphere, wallops our senses, just after the summer months? And what is Durga Puja if the shopping bug has not pricked us? Shyambazar, Hatibagan, New Market, Esplanade, Gariahat and other popular shopping destinations of Kolkata suddenly become even more crowded with bargaining customers on the pavements, chock-a-block roads and lanes, arrays of shops and markets offering lucrative sales and discounts to attract more buyers, honking vehicles and many other attractions. Yes, the swarm of people gradually rises, as more and more days pass by and Durga Puja comes closer, but it is in this crowd, one gets the sense of belonging, the spirit of Bengal. We may not enjoy the crowd, but what really makes us different from the people of other states is that we Kolkattans get united for a greater cause: the grand awe-inspiring welcome of Durga Ma and her children in our lives.

Durga Puja brings different religions, castes and people together. In those momentous five days, we forget about those invisible barriers amongst each other and revel in the happiness and enjoyment. But during these enjoyable moments, let us not forget about those who cannot afford to witness such gratification and be a part of the festivities. They are underprivileged, they are uncertain and they are deprived; deprived of our support, help and love. Durga Ma has never discriminated among her children, then why do we persist in differentiations amongst us? Caste, religion, social status and many other obstacles have always refrained us from taking the right step. But now we need to break free! It's time to uphold the spirit of Bengal and free our minds from every kind of discrimination and reach out to the impoverished and destitute ones. It's high time Bengal moved ahead.

The Other Side of Stigma

Monideepa Majumdar

IN A WORLD where many countries have opposed the idea of granting rights deserved by the LGBTQ (Lesbian, gay, bisexual, transgender and queer) community population, the Supreme Court of India has put forward a step towards the welfare of the transgender community in India.

As a citizen of West Bengal, I'm happy to notice the growing consciousness about the community, and the need for their development slowly gaining importance. Back in 2011-12, SAATHII had been trying to validate a conceptual model of the impact of the social and emotional stigma related to same-sex sexuality, transgender identity and HIV through sexually risky behaviour in West Bengal. In this survey, 73 per cent of the transgender population was from the urban areas, and the rest from suburban areas. A number of NGOs and NPOs, like Amitie Trust, Anandam, KOSHISH and PLUS Kolkata joined hands with SAATHII in this initiative. West Bengal government requested Kolkata Police to recruit transgender people in CPVC (Civic Police Volunteer Force) to provide support and employment, and to end the stigma and discrimination against the community. The appointment of Manabi Bandyopadhyay, a teacher from Vivekananda Satobarshiki Mahavidyalaya, who underwent sex-reassignment surgery in 2003, as the principal of Krishnanagar Women's College is really inspiring, as it makes her the first transgender principal of the country. In interviews with a number of newspapers, she recalled how her students have been most supportive, both at Vivekananda Satobarshiki Mahavidyalaya, where she taught for twenty years, and then in Krishnanagar Women's College, where students eagerly awaited her arrival.

In recent times, Udyami Yubak Brinda Durga Puja committee was applauded for making history with its transgender Durga idol modelled on the Ardhanarishwar. Partnering with Pratyay Gender Trust, a number of steps were taken to ensure a safe puja for the community.

All in all, the joint efforts of the government and people of West Bengal are really heartwarming, and there is hope that the whole LGBTQ community will be free from stigma in the state and outside it.

Performing Arts of Bengal

Probuddho Ganguly

শিল্প—মানুষের সুস্থ মানসিকতার সুষমামণ্ডিত বাহ্যিক প্রকাশ। পারফরমিং আর্ট অর্থাৎ একটি শিল্পের ধারা যাতে শিল্পী দর্শক বা শ্রোতার সামনে তার শিল্প নৈপুণ্য প্রকাশ করেন। গান, যাত্রা, নাটক, নাচ, কবিতা পাঠ, মুখাভিনয়, প্রভৃতি পারফরমিং আর্টের অন্তর্ভুক্ত। এই শিল্পের প্রকাশ শিল্পী কখনও একক ভাবে, কখনও অন্য শিল্পীর সহায়তাযুক্ত হয়ে তার শিল্প সুষমা প্রকাশ করে থাকেন। একটি সঙ্গীত সুগীত হবার মূলে গীতিকার ও সুরকারের অবদানও অনেকখানি। ভারতবর্ষের শিল্পের ইতিহাস বিশ্লেষণ করলে আমরা দেখতে পাই বৈদিক যুগ অর্থাৎ শ্রীঃপূঃ দুহাজার বছর থেকে পারফরমিং আর্টের শুরু। বৈদিক যুগের মূল সাহিত্য বেদ। বেদ এর সূক্তগুলির অন্য নাম শ্রুতি। কারণ এই সূক্তগুলি শ্রবণের মাধ্যমে পরম্পরাগত ভাবে গীত হত। ভারতের নাট্যশাস্ত্রে (শ্রীঃপূঃ ২য়- ৫ম শতক) আমরা পারফরমিং আর্টের অন্তর্ভুক্ত বিভিন্ন বিষয়ের তাত্ত্বিক আলোচনা আমরা পাই। শ্রীঃপূঃ ২য় শতকে ভাসের মহাভারত অবলম্বনে রচিত নাটক পঞ্চরাত্রম, শ্রীঃপূঃ ১ম শতকে মহাকবি কালিদাস বিরচিত মালবিকাগ্নিমিত্রম, অভিজ্ঞান শকুন্তলম প্রভৃতি নাটক ভারতের মঞ্চ শিল্পের প্রামাণ্য উদাহরণ। পশ্চিম বাংলা লোকায়ত জীবনের পটভূমিকায় পারফরমিং আর্টের ভূমিকা অত্যন্ত গুরুত্বপূর্ণ। এখানের পুরুলিয়া, মালদা ও পশ্চিম দিনাজপুরের ছৌ নৃত্য ও গম্ভীরা নৃত্য, মেদিনীপুরের পট শিল্প, বীরভূমের বাউল

গান, উত্তর বঙ্গের ভাটিয়ালি গান ইত্যাদি উল্লেখের দাবি রাখে। এই সমস্ত শিল্পের ধারা গুলি অনেকগুলি শিল্পের সমন্বয়ে গড়ে উঠেছে। যেমন গম্ভীরা বা ছৌ নৃত্যের ক্ষেত্রে দেখা যায় পৌরানিক কাহিনি অবলম্বনে এগুলি পরিবেশিত হয়। প্রতিটি চরিত্র নৃত্যকালীন নির্দিষ্ট মুখোশ ব্যবহার করেন। বিভিন্ন দেবদেবীর নির্দিষ্ট আয়ুধ ব্যবহার করেন। পুরুলিয়া, মালদা প্রভৃতি অঞ্চলের নৃত্য শিল্পীদের মুখোশ কে কেন্দ্র করে মুখোশ তৈরীর একটি স্বতন্ত্র শিল্প দেশে ও আন্তর্জাতিক বাজারে খ্যাতি লাভ করেছে। শিল্পের সংজ্ঞা অনুযায়ী মুখোশ শিল্প প্লাস্টিক আর্টের অন্তর্গত। কিন্তু একটি শিল্প অন্য শিল্পের পরিপূরক- তা কখন কোন কিছুর মধ্যে সীমাবদ্ধ থাকতে পারে না। শিল্প একটি দেশের জনজাতির সাংস্কৃতিক মানের সার্থক পরিচায়ক এবং আন্তর্জাতিক জগতে শিল্পের পটভূমিকায় পশ্চিম বাঙলার মান অত্যন্ত সম্মানীয় স্থানে আছে। মার্গ শিল্প এবং লোক শিল্প দুই ধারাতেই এই রাজ্য উল্লেখ্য স্থান অধিকার করেছে। পৃখিবীর বিভন্ন দেশে মার্গ শিল্পের ক্ষেত্রে আমাদের কন্ঠ ও বাদ্য শিল্পীরা নিজ নিজ ক্ষেত্রে প্রশংসার দাবি রাখেন এবং তাঁদের আনুকূল্যে বিদেশিরাও আমদের মার্গ শিল্পে আকৃষ্ট হয়েছেন ও আয়ত্ত করতে সচেষ্ট হয়েছেন। প্রসঙ্গতঃ আমজাদ আলি খান ও তাঁর সুযোগ্য পুত্রদ্বয়, নিখিল ব্যানার্জি, রাশিদ খান, তন্ময় বসু প্রভৃতির নাম উল্লেখনিও। শুধু মাত্র মার্গ সঙ্গীতই নয় রবীন্দ্রনাথ তাঁর স্বীয়কীর্তির মাধ্যমে ভারত কে বিশ্বের দরবারে পৌঁছে দিয়েছিলেন এবং ভারত এর প্রথম নোবেল প্রাপক এর সম্মান অর্জন করেছিলেন। পারফরমিং আর্ট একটি দেশের অর্থনীতিকে পরিপুষ্ট করার ক্ষেত্রে গুরুত্বপূর্ণ স্থান গ্রহণ করে। নাটক, সঙ্গীত, যাত্রা প্রভৃতি অনুষ্ঠান সাধারণতঃ কোন প্রেক্ষাগৃহে বা খোলা মঞ্চে অনুষ্ঠিত হয়। লুপ্তপ্রায় শিল্পের প্রচার করার জন্য সেই শিল্পের শিল্পীদের অনুষ্ঠানে অনশগ্রহনের জন্য আমন্ত্রন করা হয়। পশ্চিম বাংলার ক্ষেত্রে এই প্রচেষ্টা সর্বতো ভাবে প্রযোজ্য। এ ক্ষেত্রে সরকারী পৃষ্ঠপোষকতায় শিল্পের যেমন পুনরুজ্জীবন হয় তেমনই শিল্পীদের আর্থিক সনস্থান-এর পথও তৈরি হয়। পারফরমিং আর্টের মাধ্যমে একটি শিল্পের পরম্পরা বা ক্রমবিকাশ প্রকাশিত হয়। যেমন আগে বাউল শিল্পীরা মকর সংক্রান্তির সময় কেন্দুলিতে আয়োজিত বাউল মেলায়ে জমায়েত হয়ে বিভিন্ন ধারা বাউল গান করতেন। এখন

কেন্দুলিতে বাউলদের স্থায়ী আখড়া তৈরি হয়েছে। সেখানে বাউল শিল্পীরা থেকে সুরের ও ভাবের আদানপ্রদান করতে পারছেন। পারফরমিং আর্ট একটি দেশের কৃষ্টি ও সংস্কৃতির বাতাবরণ তৈরির ক্ষেত্রে অপরিহার্য ভূমিকা গ্রহণ করে। শিল্পের ধারাবাহিকতা বজায় রাখতে পারফরমং আর্টের চর্চা অপরিহার্য।

Divine Dhaak Beat

Manoj Kumar Tigga

DURGA PUJA, WHICH signifies the victory of Good over Evil, is one of the largest celebrated festivals in the world. It is also one of the biggest art exhibitions in the form of puja pandals decorated with beautiful lighting arrangements. It is celebrated from the sixth to tenth day of Ashwin month according to the Hindu calendar.

The Durga Puja celebration in India, specially Bengal, is incomplete without the beat of the dhaak—the traditional Indian drum, which is in the shape of barrel whose body is made of wood and covered with animal skin on the two ends. Durga Puja does not assume the festive mood without the magical and amazing beats of the dhaak, which the dhaakis play hanging around their necks and two thin sticks to generate the musical rhythm in form of calculated cyclic beats played in a loop. Those enchanting beats are enough to create the feel and smell of Durga Puja. The beat of the dhaak is inseparable and integral part of Durga Puja. Worship of the mother goddess is accompanied with different beats during various aspects of the Puja such as Arati, Sandhi Puja, Bisarjan, etc. The rhythm of the dhaak which requires a lot of energy, movement and sometime dancing, is a treat to watch and listen. The art of playing dhaak may appear simple, but it's not an easy task to hang that heavy drum around the neck and create divine ambience with every beat that is played during different puja rituals.

Puja rituals of Goddess Durga itself creates a mesmerising effect with melodious chants, auspicious mantras, sound of shankhas, beautiful flowers along with dhoop and incense. But it's the added flavour in the form of the beat of dhaak that takes the whole puja ceremony to an entirely different level. The dhaakis often perform barefoot with high devotion generating the divine ambience during the whole puja ceremony. The unique sound of beat produced from the dhaak forces each and everyone present around the puja place to get immersed and drenched with the puja spirit. Without the dhaak's beat, the puja spirit would be bland and incomplete.

This age old skill of playing and making the dhaak has been passed through generations serving and displaying this unique art. The dedication and effort which dhaakis display is purely magical and cannot be replaced with any other means. As the puja concludes with the Bisarjan ceremony and Goddess Durga gets submerged and sinks under water, the dhaakis along with their dhaak also go into hibernation till the next puja season. The dhaakis then wait eagerly for the next puja season to display their art once again in front of the idol of Goddess Durga.

'B' for BENGAL

Sounak Sengupta

FROM THE BLOOD-STAINED battlefields of Plassey to the vicious struggle freedom against the British; whether it is on the high-pulsating cricket grounds or in the quiet sparks of revolution born from the tip of a pen to the world of glamour and glitz of cinema—Bengal has always borne the leaders in the form of Siraj-ud-daulah, Netaji Subhash Chandra Bose, Sourav Ganguly, Rabindranath Tagore and Satyajit Ray. Flanked by the glistening snow-clad Himalayas to the deep, dangerous forests of Sunderbans, brilliant beaches of Digha and Mandarmani to the beautiful, quiet Shantiniketan—Bengal is as diverse as the Indian subcontinent itself. The state capital, once the capital of the British-ruled India, and now considered as the cultural capital, Kolkata is an unique city in itself. As Carlos Ruiz Zafón writes in *The Midnight Palace*, 'Those places where sadness and misery abound are favoured settings for stories of ghosts and apparitions.

Calcutta has countless such stories hidden in its darkness, stories that nobody wants to admit they believe but which nevertheless survive in the memory of generations as the only chronicle of the past. It is as if the people who inhabit the streets, inspired by some mysterious wisdom, realize that the true history of Calcutta has always been written in the invisible tales of its spirits and unspoken curses.'

It is a city that grows with you. It might not be the oldest or the cleanest, but it is special. As Vir Sanghvi points out, 'Calcutta is not for everyone. You want your cities clean and green; stick to Delhi. You want your cities, rich and impersonal; go to Bombay. You want them high-tech and full of draught beer; Bangalore's your place. But if you want a city with a soul: come to Calcutta.'

The whole of Bengal has a soul in itself. The green paddy fields of rural Bengal will relieve you from pollution; calm and serene Shantiniketan will cast a spell on you; the dense forests of Duars will thrill you; the first rays of the sunrise on the icy tips of the Kanchenjunga will enthral you; the historical Hazarduari of Murshidabad will enchant you—Bengal conjures up one magical place after another. After all, it is also the motherland of one of the greatest magicians, P.C. Sorcar. Bengal is a beautiful experience, putting the 'B' in 'INCREDIBLE INDIA'.

The Celebration of Home-coming

Kasturi Patra

THERE'S A FAMOUS Bengali saying, 'Bangalir baro mashe tero parbon' (loosely translated, this means that Bengalis need small reasons to celebrate and hence, for the twelve months in a year we have thirteen festivals in store). Well, I don't disagree, and I'm quite fond of this fun-loving part of our culture. Undeniably, the celebration of Durga Puja is the biggest among those festivals. For the uninitiated, it is almost a week-long festival beginning with Mahalaya, marking the home-coming of Goddess Durga and her family, concluding with the Goddess's return to her husband Lord Shiva's house in Mount Kailash on Dashami. For almost a month leading up to Durga Puja, Bengalis suffer from a bitter sweet symptom called pujo-pujo—the eager anticipation for the festivities to begin.

The smell of shiuli flower, the throngs of shoppers in Gariahat, the pandals holding promises of innovative themes, happy clouds frolicking around like fluffy sheep in the dazzling azure autumn sky, all these intensify our longing for those happy days. And then comes the auspicious Mahalaya. Since childhood, Mahalaya has held a special significance for me. Imagine, as a child, waking up at 4 a.m. to the smell of incense, accompanied by the booming voice of Birendra Krishna Bhadra on the radio chanting shlokas. Along with my siblings, I would sit near Dadubhai's lap listening to the Sanskrit phrases, and then I could feel something deep move within my core. Spirituality? I don't know what it was, but even while I type the description, my eyes well up with tears.

The spiritual experience of Mahalaya ushered in the promise of five days of undiluted fun. Be it no homework or the neighborhood drawing competitions, new clothes in the latest fashion or pandal hopping, blisters on the feet from the new pair of Sree Leathers shoes or having phuchkas at midnight; like most Bengali children, every year I'd look forward to those five days. Funnily, even after crossing thirty, I am still that ten-year-old child during Durga Puja. I still crave for the Pujorbhog, the midnight visits to Maddox Square, the new sari for the Ashtami anjali, and of course, the Puja Special Bengali magazines.

Delhi's Diwali or Mumbai's Ganesh Chaturthi fades before Bengal's Durga Puja, maybe not in terms of grandeur or scale, but surely in terms of the soul connection. I can think of very few festivals that act as such a significant catalyst to intensify the bonds within a community. The sharing of meals in the neighbourhood pandals for those five days, organizing cultural programmes, participating in rituals such as dhunuchi nach and sindur khela—these are a few ways how the people of Bengal embrace each other irrespective of caste, creed, and social status. Someone who has not soaked in the spirit of Durga Puja will never realize that a celebration can be so much deeper than just holidays, gifts, and religious ceremonies. This festival gives Bengal a special place in the world, and also in my heart.

Bengal: A Land of Contradictions

Aindrilla Chakraborty

BENGAL IS A land of contradictions. She is the silence which deafens you, yet she is the chaos, the sound of which is music to you. She is the land where the elderly discuss about the flaws in the system in absolute despair over a cup of black tea, yet she is the land where the young, vibrant, enthusiastic youth discuss how to change the system over more cups of black tea. She is the restriction that holds you back, yet she is the poetic license that helps you push through all odds to fulfil your dreams.

Bengal is the land which enriches her soul with music, yet she is the land where a talented musician has to slay his dream and give in to a settled life of an engineer or a doctor. Bengal is the land which breeds the sports culture, yet she is the land which fails to give birth to sports stars which she carries in her womb, hiding in the darkness of her slums or playing on the lush green fields of her villages. Bengal is the land wherein her children are drenched in red in the name of communal harmony, yet she is the land wherein Durga Puja and Ramzan, both are celebrated in the same spirit, by everyone. Bengal is the land which embraces change, yet she is the land which holds on to her heritage even at times of trial. She is the last drag you smoke after which you say, 'That was it. I quit.' Yet she is the Charminar you light the next moment and say, 'Oh! I miss reading Feluda stories.'

Bengal is the land which will never stop in time, which will never stop you, but she can always stop time for you. She is for everyone. But not everyone can fathom her. She can bestow her immense love on you expecting nothing in return. She shows you both; your best and your worst. She gives you a glimpse of your worst after you are done with receiving your best and she shows you your best when you are facing your worst. She shows you life. Her body is corrupt; her soul is pure. She has witnessed sins, but committed none. She is the amalgamation of old and new; the ancient and the contemporary; the traditional and the modern. She is rational. She is nostalgic. She is hope. She is despair. She is the strength. She is the weakness. She is the infant who cries innocently for help. She is the youth who has a colossal thirst of reaching the sky. She is the lover whose warm embrace comforts you. She is the mother on whose lap you can always fall back for unconditional affection and care. She is the elderly who seeks to find truce. She is the enigma which hides in her bosom, unsaid words, unexpressed emotions, dark desires and heinous secrets. She is me.

She is you. She is us. She is Bengal.

বাংলার গান

Sankhadeep Sengupta

সেই প্রথম আলাপ হয়েছিল বিদ্যার সাগরের বুকে। নৌকায় ছিলে তুমি। ছিলাম আমি। চিনলাম এ জীবন বাংলার হাতে হাত রেখে। কখনো পৌঁছেছিলাম আমরা ধানসিঁড়িটির তীরে, শঙ্খচিল, শালিকের বেশে, এক নতুন নবান্নের দেশে। কখনো রয়ে গিয়েছিলাম গানের ওপারে। নৌকার পালে হাওয়ার শব্দ থামেনি একবারও। ফুল না ফুটেও এ সকল সুভাষ দিনে হয়েছে রোজই বসন্ত। কত জোছনা কেটে গেছে তোমার সকল কথার সাথে—হেঁটেছি আমিও হাজার গল্পের ভিড়ে। দেখেছি হাজার চরিত্রের ছায়া সারি সারি। জেনেছি হুঁকোমুখো হ্যাংলারও নাকি বাংলায় বাড়ি। বর্ষার ঘন মেঘের ভাষাও শুনেছি তোমার ঠোঁটেই। লিখেছি কবিতা তোমার সাথে, ছন্দবদ্ধ মনে, ভিজেছি দুজনেই একসাথে, প্রত্যেক বাইশে শ্রাবণে। তুমিই শিখিয়েছ আমায় বিদ্রোহের গান। তোমায় নিয়েই করেছি বিপ্লবের আহ্বান। যাত্রা তো এখনো অশেষ; বন্দর বহুদূর। আরো বাকি শোনা কত সুনীল বার্তা, কত শঙ্খের সুর। মৃত্যু যদি হয়ে তোমার, থাকব ওই কবরের পাশেই. ভিজিয়ে রাখবো তোমায় দুই নয়নের জলে তিরিশ বছরেরও বেশি কাল ধরে। ফিরে আসব আবার নাহয় জাতিস্মর হয়ে। দেখবো তোমায়। চিনবো তোমার নতুন ধরণ। ইতি হোক কবির ভাষায়—'হে বঙ্গ, ভাণ্ডারে তব বিবিধ রতন'।।

Bengal Beckons You

Indranil Roy

EMBELLISHED WITH UNIQUE geographical settings the state of West Bengal extends seas of opportunities for entrepreneurs from across the world to realize their dreams. With two ports of Kidderpore and Haldia and two railways (Eastern and South-Eastern), the transportation of iron ore from Orissa and Jharkhand is hassle-free. The number 34 national highway is there as well as the road communication. In Ranigunj and Asansole there are in-built repositories of coal. The river Ganga with all her tributaries ensure a ceaseless water supply paving the way for iron and steel and heavy engineering industries. The clothing industry can once again be revived and be spread in the export industry through a sincere monitoring of the cotton and silk saris in the handloom sectors and in due course regain the lost glory. With the gorgeous Himalayan range along with her foothills, nature tourism and adventure tourism can be developed and marketed in the domestic and international markets. Rock climbing, mountaineering, white-water rafting, mountain biking, skiing are the few of the biggest draws among the adventure lovers. Ski-resorts, nature camps and visits to the exotic indigenous cultures of mountain tribes ignites the inquisitiveness of culture lovers. Witnessing the exotic flora and fauna of Himalaya are a treat for nature lovers. Travelling through the plains of Terai region breathing the remnants of mountain topography enable the general tourist to feel the pulse of mountain tourism.

Moving south wandering through the districts of Malda the traveller gets a taste of religious and historical tourism while exploring the ruins of the Hindu era of the Middle Age and marvelling at the reminiscences of Bengal's last Muslim monarchy in Murshidabad. Nadia reverberates with the omnipresence of the great reformer Chaitanyadeb and his Vaishnava movement. Added to this is a cultural overtone of wonderful pottery of Krishananagar.

Then the traveller finds himself among the unique terracotta ruins of temples of Bankura and Bishnupur, the architecture, murals of which offer experiences to be cherished for a lifetime. When the traveller enters Kolkata, the capital of the state with her panorama of 300 years of history merged with different cultures along with the suburbs of Uttarpara, Chandernagore and Bandel offering their shares of much older historical lineage. In the final leg of his journey, the traveller soothes his eyes by looking at the vast blues of the Bay of Bengal while loitering on the beaches of Sankarpur and New Digha. But while exploring the Sunderban forest range, our friend gets the unique taste of the world's largest mangrove forest along with the Royal Bengal Tiger, the most beautiful and majestic of the species in the world.

With the snow-clad mountain range in the north, the plains in the middle and the sea-side deltas in the south are few of the most sought-after locales for the film industry. The availability of the cheapest and most efficient manpower is a bliss for industry. Dear entrepreneur, what are you waiting for? Come to West Bengal, where the heart is.

Chromatic Bengal

Swastika Bandyopadhyay

THE MORNING WAS marked by a shrill whistle of the train approaching Howrah station. Bengal was a whole new world to her. Her family returned to their native motherland after thirty long years. She came during the time when the city like a drunken boat danced to the rhythms of the beating drums and the overpowering incense of dhuno.

'Mother has finally arrived!' someone shouted on the streets, while people with ruddy faces moved about her and her family. She was picking up her luggage to dump in the dickey behind taxi. It was an early morning tour, and thus, she saw Kolkata awakening.

Ganga's ghat brimmed with people worshipping her and Twinkle steadily turned her head to the fearless kids jumping in the river; and somewhere deep inside she believed that the calmness of the Ganga is motherly. She saw the stalls opening, while the sun like the ever glowing crimson ball rose like the proud face of a soldier. Twinkle's grandma told her all sorts of fanciful things that she never saw in Pune, Delhi or Hyderabad, and all were somehow so very different from Bengal.

Bengal to her always meant home; its inexplicable closeness to her heart was strange in itself. Twinkle remembered how her grandma's face lit up while talking about the Durga Puja, Laxmi Puja, Saraswati Puja, which fascinated her very much. Twinkle always wanted to look like a queen draped in her yellow silk sari. She stopped her taxi, got out to see Victoria Memorial and watched it stand in a grand fashion with its head held up high kissing the sky, its cherubim like crown adorned her forehead with an angel blowing the trumpet. Newspapers, flower stalls, paan shops, fish markets all stood sturdy against the green background and the soothing songs of Manna Dey, Kishore, Hemant. Then she heard a tuneful song from a nearby tea stall, 'Shaat ti bochhor aage.' She asked her mother whose voice it was.

Mother took a deep sigh and with an air of triumph and replied quietly, 'Jaganmoy Mitra' and then she became silent. She remembered how dearly their beloved grandma heard this austere man's voice echoing through their palatial house in Baghbazar and how she melancholically wiped her husband's frame, as if trying to awaken him from his deep, eternal slumber. She sang songs of Sandhya and Lata with her melodious voice and how she was believed to be so enterprising even at the age of seventy-four. She read the books penned by Rabindranath Tagore, Sarat Chandra, Rishi Bankim, Narayan Ganguly, Tarashankar Bandyopadhyay, Sunil Gangopadhaya, Saradendu Bandyopahya, Sanjeev Chattopadhyay, Subhod Ghosh and Lila Majumdar.

Twinkle remembers how her grandma got her books from the book fair and how ardently she invited her each Holi and Durga Puja, but somehow she was busy in her life in the alien state which didn't allow her any holidays. But she swore to come to see her someday; today she came but only granny was no longer there.

Everything else remained in chromatic Bengal.

Bengal—The Land of Culture

Dahlia Ghosh

PICTURE YOURSELF IN a vibrant land, pulsating with life, where spirits have not been dampened by the monotones of existence, where people are not afraid to stand up for a cause. Where opinionated arguments strike up with ease, whether in philosophical discussions over tea-cups and newspapers, or mass hue and cry raised by multitudes on streets, rallying for a larger purpose. Where blind pursuit of material pleasures has not weakened the links to their cultural heritage. Where each child is taught at least one form of fine art in his early years. Where elders are still respected and their blessings sought before every new venture. Where the fish-loving soft-spoken dhoti-kurta clad Babu and the jhola-laden idealistic poet-politician in a coffee shop of yesteryear, morphs effortlessly into the smart young professional of today. Where the native reaches out to his roots every year when his homeland, bathed in the serene golden light of autumn and the early-morning fragrance of dewdrops and Shiuli, pulsates with spiritual splendour and Ma Durga, the fiery warrior against evil and the benevolent mother of four, is fondly welcomed to her home like a girl by her family. Where small pairs of feet painted on red floors with rice powder, lead the way indoors for the Goddess of Wealth to bless the household. Where winding roads of brick-red earth, accompanied by rustic folk-tunes or serene Rabindrasangeet, lead the way to suburbs with children engaged in gully-cricket or frenzied collection of mangoes in the wake of an ensuing monsoon storm. Where football matches between two leading teams lead to hysterical outbursts of staunch supporters. Where it is mandatory for families, complete with hold-alls and monkey caps, to visit at least one tourist destination a year.

This is the land of Rabindranath and Bankim and Netaji and Rammohan, the land where tradition merges with modernization, where the sound wisdom of the past paves the way for a promising future. This is Bengal, the land of culture.

Bangla Gaan: A Buffet of Wonders

Proiti Seal Acharya

'BIKHHOBE BIPLOBE TOMAAKE chai, bhishon oshombhobe tomake chai, Shanti oshantite tomake chai, Ei bibhrantite tomake chai.' These lines from the iconic Kabir Suman song seem to express perfectly what Bengalis feel for music. Whether it is the radio at the neighborhood corner paan shop, or the CD player in the car or a packed concert at Nazrul Manch, Bengalis never seem to have enough of music. Bengal is the birthplace of so many varied genres of music that it is almost impossible to keep count. The listener traverses many a path in his journey through this ever evolving universe accompanying Lalon in his eternal quest for the Baul's 'Moner Manush', joining in the chorus of a Kabigaan at a musical debate, extracting new meaning from Tagore's compositions at each of life's stages, celebrating the arrival of new love in the mellifluous, evergreen songs of the 60's and 70's, and finding a voice for his disillusionment with urban life in the work of Mohiner Ghoraguli. This listener, enthralled, continues into the world of the legend, singer-songwriter Kabir Suman, who showed what Bengali music could be when it was both rooted to its indigenous heritage, and responsive to the world at large. Fellow artists such as Moushumi Bhowmick, Nachiketa and many others have also made indelible marks on this universe. The listener, now, is spoiled for choice. Is it Jibonmukhi or Adhunik gaan that he wants, masterfully performed by artists such as Lopamudra Mitra or Subhamita, or does he want Puratoni Bangla gaan with fresh musical arrangements, presented by young, upcoming artists like Payel Kar? Does he want to say 'Amake amar moto thakte dao', taking refuge in his postmodern solitude, or contemplating whether he might suggest to his lover 'Chol rastay shaji tram line, ar kobitay shue couplet'? Does he want to delve deep into the many forms of Bengali folk music that have recently witnessed a revival in popularity? The Bhatiyaali songs of the boatmen in the many rivers of Bengal, or the emotionally charged strains of the Bhawaiiya are capable of moving the 21st century Bengali to tears. The 'Bangla Band' has also seen exciting development in the recent past. The listener can enjoy the effervescent soundscape of Chandrabindu while simultaneously reflecting on their subtle social commentary. He can find release from the vagaries of everyday life through the music of Fossils or Cactus.

The Bengali listener develops an ear for good music from the time of his childhood, when his mother puts him to sleep with 'Ghumparani mashi pishi'. He falls in love with Tagore the moment he learns 'Phule phule dhole dhole', and the radio becomes his gateway to discover the other genres. Now, with the dynamic expansion of the Internet, listeners of Bengali music have the opportunity to appreciate music from the other Bengal as well. This allows for artistic communication and collaboration between musicians in West Bengal and Bangladesh, with the promise of new and exciting directions for Bengali music.

Kolkata

Prakalpa Bhattacharya

হাতে যদি একটা একটু দামী ক্যামেরা থাকে, তাহলে খুব সহজে ভীড় টানা যায়। এই যেমন ওই বিদেশী মানুষটা। সকালে শিয়ালদা সাউথ স্টেশনের চলতি ভীড়ের মাঝখানে ফটো তুলছে ছোট ছোট ছেলেগুলোর, যারা ওই চত্বরেই থাকে, খায়, ঘুমোয়। ছেলেগুলো মজা পাচ্ছে, কেউ কেউ পোজ ও দিচ্ছে। হঠাত লোকটা ফটো তোলা ছেড়ে কী যেন খুঁজতে লাগলো। তাইতো, একটু আগে ওর পিঠে একটা ব্যাগ ছিল না? কোথায় গেল? নামিয়ে রেখেছে? নাঃ, নেই। লোকটা এবার বিচলিত, ব্যাগটা এদিক ওদিক খুঁজছে। ওর কথা যারা বুঝছে তারাও পাত্তা দিচ্ছে না। ওই তো একজন রেল পুলিশ। ব্যাগে নাকি ওর টাকা ছাড়াও পাসপোর্ট, আর টিকিট, আজ সন্ধ্যেবেলা কোথায় যাবে যেন... না, পাত্তা দিল না পুলিশটা। থানায় গেলে ডাইরিও করা যাবে না নাকি। লোকটা চিন্তিত মুখে বসে আছে। ফোনটাও বোধহয় ওই ব্যাগে ছিল। গায়ে টি শার্ট আর ঢোলা হাফপ্যান্ট। হাতে ক্যামেরাটা সম্বল। একটা ছোট ছেলে এসে ওকে কী বললো, ও তার সঙ্গে চললো। কোথায় যাচ্ছে? দেখি তো! শিয়ালদহ নর্থের সামনে দিয়ে, লেবুওয়ালাদের পাশ কাটিয়ে... শিশির মার্কেটের ভিতরে, একটা সেলুনে। এখানে কী কাজ! একজন দাড়ি কামাচ্ছে চোখ বন্ধ করে। ছেলেটা তাকে কী বলল, সে একবার চোখ খুলে বিদেশীটাকে দেখল। আবার চোখ বন্ধ করে কী উত্তর দিল। কোন ভাষায়? বিদেশীটা মাথা নাড়ছে,

বুঝে, নাকি না বুঝেই! পাশের একটা দোকানদার বিদেশীটাকে একটা শালপাতায় কচুরি আর তরকারী খেতে দিল। আহা বেচারার খিদে পেয়েছিল, হাসি মুখে নিয়ে খেতে আরম্ভ করলো। ছোট মিনারেল ওয়াটারের বোতল বাড়িয়ে দিল একজন। এরা কি সবাই জেনে গেছে যে লোকটার সর্বস্ব চুরি হয়ে গেছে? মাথা নেড়ে নেড়ে কী বলছে ও সকলকে, দু জন হাসছে শুধু। স্টেশন আগের থেকেও ব্যস্ত। খুব লক্ষ্য না করলে ভীড়ের মধ্যে কারো চোখেও পড়বে না বিদেশীটাকে। এখন ও ক্যাসেটের দোকানগুলোর সামনে। গান শোনবার মুড আছে ওর এখন! মনে হচ্ছে যেন অপেক্ষা করছে কারো। কোনো বন্ধু? পুলিশ? তবে বিদেশীটার নার্ভ খুব শক্ত, মানতেই হবে। হাউ-হাউ করে কই ভেঙে পড়েনিতো! বেলা দুপুর গড়িয়ে গেল... ভীড়ের রঙ বদলাচ্ছে। ফলওয়ালাগুলো রোদুর বাঁচাতে উড়ালপুলের নীচে ঢুকে বসেছে। ঠেলাওয়ালা গুলোর চিল্লানি কমে এসেছে। বিদেশীটার বোতলের জল শেষ, এদিক ওদিক তাকাচ্ছে। চাইতেও পারছে না, আবার যে কোন জল খেতে সাহসও পাচ্ছে না... বাহ রে, ওই ঘোলওয়ালা এক গ্লাস লস্যি দিল লোকটাকে! ওকি... ওখানে কিসের জটলা? এদিকেই আসছে, বিদেশীটাকেই খুঁজছে। এই রে, মারধোর করবে নাকি! হ্যাঁ, ওকে ঘিরেই দাঁড়ালো সবাই, আর... আরে, ওই তো, ওইতো লোকতার ব্যাগটা! লোকতার চোখ মুখের চেহারা বদলে গেছে... কী সব বলছে হাউ হাউ করে, হাত জড়িয়ে ধরে... কিছু বোধহয় বার করে ছেলেগুলোকে দিতে গেল... টাকা... আর কী... না নিল না কেউ... এবার চলে যাচ্ছে সকলে... বিদেশীটা ব্যাগটা খুলে দেখছে সবকিছু আছে কি না। আছে, নিশ্চিন্ত হয়ে তাকালো এতক্ষণ পর। লোকটা পিঠে ব্যাগ নিয়ে ধীরে ধীরে হেঁটে আসছে আবার শিয়ালদহ নর্থের দিকে। ওর ট্রেন ক টায়? নিশ্চয়ই সময় আছে এখনো। সকালে যাদের ফটো তুলেছিল, তারা হাত নাড়ল লোকটাকে দেখে। লোকটাও হাত নাড়ল। বিদায় কলকাতা!

Where Dreams Grow!

Tiasa Banerjee

AS AN EIGHT-YEAR-OLD girl, I really did not want to leave the beauties and mysteries of my birth place to come to Kolkata, a city I considered chaotic, over-populated and simply too noisy to suite a quiet girl. It just so happened that the city drew me in and made me one of its own. The city gave chaos a new meaning. Today, after having travelled to many parts of West Bengal, the only word I can use to describe the state is 'vibrant'.

Everywhere I go I can see people mingling together—topics ranging from politics to cricket, opening of a new boutique next door to the shop selling low quality products. Somehow, people here grow up among such diversity that being 'different' ceases to matter. Diversity can be seen when you leave your room in search of an evening snack. Every locality seems to have its resident biriyani, momo, Mughlai, tandoori and pani-poori stall. People crowd around these shops, waiting for their parcels to be delivered, talking to each other in languages and dialects unrecognizable to the common ear.

Diversity can be seen when you go to someone's house and see the the mistress of the house discussing the next door Bramhin girl's marriage to her Japanese lover with her maid-servant like old-time friends. Marriage is another point of notice in West Bengal. From where I stand, the dowry system seems non-existent. Love marriages among different linguistic groups and castes is common, at least among the Kolkatans, and is seen as a basis to expand their cultural knowledge.

Cultural knowledge is something that indeed is common between all Bengalis. I am yet to see a Bengali man who can stay in one place for over a year. A trip to the uncharted areas is a must. I am yet to see a Bengali girl who has not been trained in singing, dancing or acting from her early years. West Bengal produces some of the best artists in India every year. A West Bengal born child is lucky indeed. Instead of having single-minded focus on the competitive world, she grows up learning from experiences. She grows up in an atmosphere of education intermingled with art. Even after ten years, West Bengal does not cease to amaze me. It is developing so fast. The barren lands are being converted into corporations, cottage industries are being set up, modern technology has already reached so many villages.

It is so amazing that it thrills me to be part of this growth. It thrills me to be part of a great legacy of Indian legends.

Whenever I face a problem that terrifies me, my mother reminds me, 'A girl born in the land of Vivekananda must know to overcome fear.' West Bengal is not yet our haven of dreams, it is the place where dreams are built; that place which was bathed in blood for India's freedom. West Bengal is beautiful.

Inspiration

Aritra Basu

THE WRITER'S BLOCK had continued for more than a month now. Pen set against paper bore words, surely, but the old poignance, lucidity and elegance was nowhere to be found. His characters were now two-dimensional, without a fate hanging over their heads or a motive driving them from place to place. Amitav, the Booker prize-winner, hailing from south Bengal, was sure that he would be following the footsteps of Wordsworth, and would turn into a barren mind after turning fifty. Black ink that poured forth from the fountain pen appeared to him like everything wrong he had ever done in his life, and a creator as he was, the white sheets seemed to be representative of his blank mind.

A thorough knowledge of the streets of north Kolkata, a perceptive ear for the tram horns and an innate capability to put beautiful words next to each other had made his novels as popular as they are. The publishers, on the other hand, relentless as destiny, constantly reminded him of the aggressive deadline for his next novel. He was out of ideas and excuses with which to defer them. It took him quite long to realize what had gone wrong with him since the last novel. Urban life was always Amitav's forté. The din and bustle of the city, the mundane chores always gave him a pleasure beyond words. This time around, he knew it for a fact that urban life had given him four consecutive successes, and it was now time to pen down the struggles of rural people.

On a day full of sunlight, the writer took a detour from his regular walk in the obscure village and decided to visit a decrepit hut. The owner talked to him like he belonged there, and from that conversation, Amitav learned a lot. Returning to his temporary house in the village, he saw with astonishment his pen recreate the old magic for which readers all across the globe love and admire him. A sense of acknowledgement seeped deep in his blood. He owed the people of the village the success of the book which he knew would go on to be another feather in his cap. However, for a long time he could not decide how he would pay them back. Two ideas ran simultaneously in his head. The end of the day saw both of them executed.

The book was released first in Kolkata, the closest metropolitan to the village of Madhyamgram so that the invited people could join in the release with ease, and the dedication of the book read: 'To the people of Madhyamgram who taught me how Bengal still manages to inspire and teach you in times of utter distress.'

Requiem for the City of Joy

Rajeswari Dasgupta

EVERY DAY, AS I battle adulthood in my city, I constantly encounter people who exclaim derisively, West Bengal no longer has a culture. These people either imply that the glorious past has been vindictively eradicated by the youth of today, or that we are too rustic, too mundane to be awarded the accolade of culture. I strongly disagree. Not only because sociologically, culture simply denotes a way of life, and not the differentiating, stratifying instrument it is utilized as today, to closet and confine to timeless oblivion those societies which the group of so-called intellectuals patronizingly declare as uncultured; but because as a college student who is immersed in the very soul of this city, I know definitively, that Kolkata (and West Bengal by that extension) retains its culture beautifully.

I see it every time I discuss with loud, unafraid words everything that perplexes me about the world with my friends outside college, with the quintessential ordinariness of a cup of cha. I embrace it in the morning Metro, with the crowded milieu of everyday consternation, of office-goers who rush like unbounded flocks the moment the doors open at Rabindra Sadan. I feel it in the Ladies Compartment of Bandel Local at 8 o'clock at night amidst women who persevere in their workplace far from home, and either bid adieu to the people they love or wait anxiously for the comfort of home. I can almost taste it in Nizam's and Nahoum's, as Esplanade in all its classical magnificence welcomes me with open arms and red-brick walls. It immerses me in Bagbazar Ghat as the Ganges goes on forever, peaceful, sentient but indifferent to generations of the population who drown their sorrows in its waters.

It overwhelms me as I sit surrounded by theatre, art and splendour at Nandan and the Nandikar Theatre Festival awes me to my very core. I dance to it softly and self-consciously in the retro music of Someplace Else and with all my soul when the dhol plays the archetypal beats that welcome Pujo with days and nights where all the lives in Kolkata gracefully collide and separate, when, for those few days, this city acknowledges us indistinguishable, irrevocable pieces of its soul.

I experience it with Bauls in Shantiniketan, who lose themselves in their music as I lose myself in the broken, frozen trees of the Khoai. I can hear it in kind words a stranger recites in my ear as I seek comfort in unfamiliar roads. I am surrounded by the City of Joy, with its colours and its laughter and its faded loveliness that does not fail to make me catch my breath, and there is no place I'd rather be than here. So, I say to all those individuals who labour under the sad delusion that my city and my state is empty of culture: Open your eyes. This is a haven, a living, breathing, dynamic pulse of a city, where culture is born and bred and never dies.

Torchbearer of Indian Cinema

Sumanto Sengupta

BENGALI FILMS HAVE always been the torchbearer of Indian cinema. Starting from the early 20th century, Bengali cinema has produced quite a few luminaries who have made immense contribution on the world stage. Be it Hiralal Sen, Promothesh Baruah, B.N. Sircar, Satyajit Ray, Ritwik Ghatak, Mrinal Sen, or Tapan Sinha to name a few who have been masters in their own way in giving Bengali cinema a new idiom.

The 50's to 70's were considered to be the golden period of Bengali cinema which saw the birth of some legendary actors like Chhabi Biswas, Pahari Sanyal, Bikash Roy, Bhanu Banerjee, Johor Roy, Robi Ghosh and Anup Kumar. Even Actresses who shone during the golden era were Chhaya Devi, Arundhati Devi, Manju De, and Molina Devi, whose performances were also appreciated by the audience. However, two actors who were the standard bearers of Bengali cinema during the golden age were Uttam Kumar and Soumitra Chatterjee. The former was the most popular commercial hero who took acting to new heights. The latter, however, is one of the most renowned and prolific actors not only in Bengal but in the world and whose films have received high accolades from the world fraternity. The noted actresses who made their presence felt with some memorable performances included Suchitra Sen, Supriya Devi, Madhabi Mukherjee, Tanuja, Sharmila Tagore, Aparna Sen, and Mamata Shankar, which are still etched in memories of the film loving audience.

During the late 70's bengali cinema did go through a slump as good movies were hard to come by. Quite a few remakes made the rounds of the cinema halls which were shabby and of poor cinematic value and quality. If we notice carefully, then we can state emphatically that the quality of Bengali cinema was of very high standards during the 50's, 60's and 70's. The films made during this period not only earned national awards but also made a name for themselves in different world festivals. The 80's also had notable films which were taken note of by the world audience but they were very few in number. Things however started looking up in the early 90's with the advent of a new breed of films made by the likes of Aparna Sen, Rituparno Ghosh, Goutam Ghosh, and Buddhadeb Dasgupta, which came as a breath of fresh air. Bengali films again started ruling the roost in the national awards arena as well as making rounds in the world circuit. Many pathbreaking films were made by talented makers who were responsible in carrying forward the rich legacy of Bengali cinema.

The last decade again was witness to some highly intelligent films made by some prolific and great film-makers who have mastered the craft of storytelling which has always been the strength of Bengali films. These film-makers are ably supported by the government of the day which is a very welcome sign during this age of piracy. Quite a few studios have been renovated and given a new look which is of utmost importance in producing well-made films. Hence, it could be said that Bengali films are once more flourishing and making their presence felt with the full support of the governmental machinery. The show must go on!

ঝক্কাস

Tandrima Bhattacharya Chatterjee

বাইপাসে গাড়ীর ভীড়ে দাঁড়িয়ে ছটফট করছি; বইমেলার ভীড়ে সব গাড়ী আটকে; ড্রাইভার বললো- 'সাব জি, ঝক্কাস জ্যাম। ঘুমিয়ে নিন। "বরকে বললুম "ঝক্কাস মানে তার মানে বিরক্তিকর, তাই তো? "বর বসন্তের হালকা হাসিমাখা চোখে বললে," উঁহু। বাজারের মাছওলাও বলেছে, 'দাদা, নিয়ে যান পাবদা। ঝক্কাস আছে।'" বাংলা অভিধানে এখনো ব্রাত্য, কিন্তু দৈনন্দিন ওঠাবসায় তার অনায়াস যাতায়াত। সে ঝক্কাস। আমার ক্লাস টেনের ছাত্র উল্লাস চাপতে না পেরে তার বন্ধুকে বলেই ফেললো, "ঝক্কাস চুল কেটেছিস, বস।" আমি এ্যাটেডেন্স রেজিস্টার হাতে নিয়মানুবর্তিতা আর নতুন Register এরদোদুল্যমানতায় গম্ভীর মুখে, তরল মনে ক্লাসে ঢুকি। "এটা কি চুল কেটেছিস? দাঁড়া, গার্জেন কল করব।" পিছন থেকে শুনতে পাই" ম্যাম, নেইমারকে দেখেন নি?" শুনেও না শোনার ভান করে নামডাকা শেষ করে বলি, "নেইমারের মত খেলতে পারবি? আগে ওর মতো হ' তারপর ওমন চুল কাটবি।" দ্বিধাগ্রস্ত ছেলেমানুষেরা মুখ বন্ধ করে ফেলে উপযুক্ত উত্তর না পেয়ে।আর আমিও কপিবুক স্টাইলে খেলে ক্লাস কন্ট্রোল করে ফেলেছি এই ভেবে নিজেকে বললাম, "বাহ।" ওমা!! আমার "বাহ" আমার কানে ফিরে এল "ঝক্কাস" হয়ে। তাকিয়ে দেখলাম কে বলল কথাটা? সবাই লিখছে। তার মানে শেষে আমিই? মস্তিষ্কে রাসায়নিক সাম্যে গন্ডগোল! মুন্নাভাই এর কথায় কেমিক্যাল

লোচা। ক্রমশ আমি দেখছি আমার চারপাশ পুরোমাত্রায় ঝক্কাস হয়ে উঠছে। ট্রাভেল এজেন্ট 'ঝক্কাস' অফার দিচ্ছে; ঘরের দেওয়ালে ডিজাইনার পেন্ট দেখে কাজের মাসির মুখে 'ঝক্কাস' হাসি; ইলেক্ট্রিশিয়ান তালকানা টিউবের তাল ঠিক করে বলে," এবার ঝক্কাস জ্বলছে।"; পাড়ার ছেলের কাছে পাড়ার পুজো প্যান্ডেল—"পুরো ঝক্কাস"; তবে ঝক্কাস এর গতি কিন্তু সর্বত্রগামী নয়। বৃষ্টি এলে যারা মাখায় পলিব্যাগ আটকে আপনার আমার বাড়ি কাগজটা ঠিক সময়ে পৌঁছে দেয়, তার হার না মানা জীবনযুদ্ধে, সেই মুহূর্তের স্বস্তি আর সৌন্দর্যবোধকে খুঁজে পাবেন এই 'ঝক্কাস' নামক শব্দটিতে। এখনো ভদ্রলোকের ড্রয়িংরুমের বাইরে ঝক্কাস হাওয়াই চটি পরে দাঁড়িয়ে আছে। অপেক্ষা বসন্তের সমীরণ কখন দরজা খুলবে, আর সে সামাজিক ডিগ্নীলাভ করে ঢুকে পড়বে ভদ্রলোকের ড্রয়িংরুমে। সেদিন সাব জি, মেমসাহেবের গলায় রবি ঠাকুরের গান শুনে—না, unparallel বা awesome নয়—বলে উঠবেন—"ঝক্কাস"।

The Perfect Getaway

Kanishka Chakrabarty

ASK AN AVERAGE Indian what comes to his mind at the mention of Bengal, and he is most likely to say Sourav Ganguly, Mithun Chakraborty, Rabindrasangeet, and bhodrolok and bhodromohila who are well acquainted and, perhaps, quite proficient in the field of arts and literature, and so on. All of these are of course apt; as a non-resident Bengali, I can vouch for the Bengaliness of most to varying degrees, but the truth is that there's no single thing that makes West Bengal so special, and to limit it to a list would be committing a folly. Indeed, it's the potpourri of all these and other innumerable factors that make Bengal and Bengalis stand out.

It's been close to two decades that I no longer reside in my state, my visits are now limited to important family occasions and of course, Durga Puja; but every time I go, I find Bengal has been waiting for me like a patient lover with forgiving, open arms. It's as if I have never left, yet no matter how long my stay is, it always seems too short, passing by in a flash before I can soak up the experience. I feel my heart go heavy when the hour of return arrives, and no amount of sandesh and chanachur in my backpack can make up for the separation. That is precisely where Bengali literature comes into play.

Whenever I miss Bengal too much, I know that arguably the state's greatest legacy and contribution—the works of a long list of acclaimed writers—are never out of reach. I pick up a random book written in Bengali, and in an instant, I am home. The sight of villagers ploughing their land as a train rambles on in the distance, the smell of mango leaves, the taste of the delicious hilsa, the cacophony of arguments over football, the shiuli flower, the dhunuchi naach during Durga Puja, the clouds as dark as death in the evenings; it's all there for the taking. All you need to do is leaf through a few pages. It doesn't matter when the book was written, or how old you are. There's a timelessness to the literature of Bengal, and these books have aged better than the finest of whiskies.

I hope that someday, not too long from now, I will be back where I belong, for good; relishing the sights, sounds, and tastes of Bengal like I have never before; without the need of constantly looking at the calendar and counting days I have left before I have to pack my bags. But, until then, I rely on my collection of Bengali books for my almost perfect getaways.

Chai Gorom Chai!

Kasturi Dasgupta

'CHAI GOROM CHAI!'; 'Eksho eksho takar saree!'; 'Ghoti-gorom!'; 'Aat-anar kola!' Nowhere but here in Bengal do we hear such a cacophony of voices when we travel through the length and breadth of the state. The creativity of the calls to potential customers is as diverse as the products offered from the humble tea to the complex phones! Be it on the pavements of New Market or the trains to Shantiniketan or buses to Salt Lake Sector V, these calls not only mark the spirit of human ingenuity but also an art form of the highest order. Some calls are so complex that though they are difficult to decipher, they immediately attract attention. These rhapsodies are uniquely worded, practiced and require a profound amount of stamina to belt them out throughout the day. The calls are as specific to individuals and their trade as painting strokes of any artist. They are vocal heirlooms that are passed on from generation to generation. As society marches forward this way of life is fast disappearing along with the calls to humble consumerism. Very few realize that these hawkers provide a hot meal when there is none else to be had, a comforting smile on a tired return journey and a burst of enthusiasm for life that does not wane from dawn to dusk.

Story of Football

Sandeep Dutta

CRICKET AND FOOTBALL are two of the most popular sports of Bengal. Football, after hearing this word, Bengalis experience an energetic feeling—like they will be ready to play in any kind of weather. From a pre-schooler to an old man everybody loves to play and watch football. We have the best national clubs, Mohun Bagan, East Bengal and Mohammedan Sporting Club. There is a continuous rivalry among us for Mohun Bagan and East Bengal like for Barcelona and Real Madrid. We may remain unrewarded with trophies but the passion for football remains unbeatable which creates this vibrancy.

Salt Lake Stadium is the world's second largest stadium. Our clubs can easily draw more than one lakh spectators in domestic matches, whereas even in international matches it will be difficult to find that passion for football. Our own country may not be counted among the top 100 teams but our passion for the game will top in every aspect. Football was famous before Indian independence also.

British soldiers, sailors and traders introduced different kinds of sports in the whole of Bengal. Even before the formation of FIFA, East India Company organized football matches all over Bengal. Local institutions encouraged the young minds of our community which lead to the formation of Kolkata League and IFA Shield games. Everybody in Bengal remembers that historic match between Mohun Bagan and East Youker (a British regimental team) in 1911 where Mohun Bagan won the match. It was an epic match like India winning over British and the Mohun Bagan flag sailing over Fort William. The All India Football Federation (AIFF) came into existence in 1937. Before AIFF, Indian Football Association sent a football team to Java. It was the first official tour abroad by IFA, in 1933, under the captainship of legendary Gosto Paul whose statue has been installed in Maidan, Kolkata.

Football's popularity has been largely due to the fact that football fans established their loyalties among three big clubs, Mohun Bagan, Mohammedan Sporting and East Bengal. Players of these clubs became heroes to their millions of supporters. Mohammedan Sporting Club, though its popularity was mainly confined to Muslim supporters, reached out to Hindu players, with many of them becoming keen on donning its jerseys. The partition of Bengal led to people of West Bengal becoming supporters of Mohun Bagan and people who migrated from Bangladesh into ardent backers of East Bengal.

Bengal Always Ahead

Suvadip Ghosh

THE FACT THAT Facebook and Rupa has chosen Bengal among other states as the first initiative of this kind is a testimony in itself that there is a lot to be written about Bengal. It is really difficult to choose any one subject while writing about Bengal as it has contributed to sports, music, culture, history, politics, films, education…what not?

To start off, Bengal has given our country so many historical and political figures: Subhash Chandra Bose, Aurobindo, Surjo Sen, Chittaranjan Das, Vivekananda to name a few and even the current president of our country Mr Pranab Mukherjee. I take pride in the fact that names like Rabindranath Tagore, Bankim Chandra Chattopadhay, Sarat Chandra Chatterjee and Jibanondo Das, were from Bengal, who contributed so much to our culture. Even our education system is indebted to these great men as numerous stories, novels and poems were written by them.

And that reminds me that India's National Song and Anthem were contributed by poets from Bengal.

That brings me to other subjects—films and music.

Here also we boast of stalwarts like Kishore Kumar, Sachin and Rahul Deb Barman, Manna Dey, Hemant Kumar and Salil Chowdhury who sang/produced numerous memorable songs, tunes that are played and listened to even today and will be played for generations to come. They also inspired several generations who adored them, produce soulful music. As far as films are concerned, the maestro Satyajit Ray, winner of Oscar for Lifetime Achievement and maximum number of National Awards (including all departments of his films), had put Bengal right there on top in the world of cinema. Not to forget Mrinal Sen, Goutam Ghosh, Rituporno Ghosh, Tapan Sinha, who had won several awards and acclaim across the world in several film festivals and in our country as well. Popular film stars of yesteryears like Biswajeet Charkaverty, Ashok Kumar, Jaya Bhaduri, Rakhi are also from this lovely state named Bengal.

As far as theatre/performing arts are concerned, we have Girish Ghosh, Shambhu Mitra, Utpal Dutt, who were stalwarts in these fields. To talk about sports, we take pride in mentioning Sourav Ganguly, P.K. Banerjee, Chuni Goswami, Leander Pae,s and Anirban Lahiri who is the No. 1 golfer in India. We have century-old famous clubs like East Bengal, Mohun Bagan and Mohamadan Sporting

Club and numerous clubs. We also have Eden Gardens and Salt Lake

Stadium, which are known as the Mecca in India for cricket and football respectively.

As far as I know, Kolkata has several esteemed clubs like Calcutta Club, Saturday Club, Tolly Club, CCFC and many other clubs that few states can boast of, where events and recreation happen every day.

There is something about Bengal that has attracted Mother Teresa, Usha Uthup and many others who are not from Bengal to make Bengal their Home.

Ami Banglai gaan gaai,
Ami Banglar gaan gai
Ami amar amake ei Banglai khuje pai

সোহাগ

Prabir Biswas

সোহাগ, তু ক্যাইমোন আছিস রে বিটি? আগে তবু থক্কোর পাঠাইতিস। ইক্ষোন তুয়ার কোনো থক্কোর পাইচ্ছি না। আমি জানি, তুয়ার বাপের উপ্পর রাইগ হইছে, অভিমোন হইছে। সিইইই সাত বচ্ছর পানা বয়েসে সীতামোণি তুয়ারে লিয়া গ্যালো কইলকাত্তা। বাবুদের বাড়ীর কাজ দিবেক বইল্যে। তখ্খণ তু খুব কেইন্দে ছিলি, বাপকে ছেড়ে, মা টকে ফেইল্যে, ছুট ভাই টকে ফেইল্যে যেতে চাস লাই তুই। জোর কইরে পাঠায়ছিলম তুকে। তখ্খণ আমাইদের খুব অভাব। পিঁপড়ার ডিম থাইচ্ছি কুনো দিন তো কুনো দিন বন ওল সেদ্ধ কইরে থাচ্ছিলম বটে। ই জঙ্গল মহল তখ্খণ খুদ্দার আগে ঘোইলছে। কারু ঘরে দানা পানি লাই। জল টা পোরয়োস্ত উ দুরের গেরামের ইঁদারা থেইকে আইনতে হোতো। তুয়ার মা তাপ উঠার আগে চইল যেত জল আইন্তে। এক ঘড়া জল দিয়ে চালায় লিতাম পিয়াস আর খুদ্দা। সিতো পেরায় দশ বচ্ছোর কাল হোইলো। তু এখন বেশ ডাগগোর পানা হইচ্ছিস লিশ্চয়? তুয়ার মুখটা খুব মইনে পড়ে রে সোহাগী। তু আয় একবারটি বাপের কাচ্ছে। তুয়াকে একবারটি দেখি মা। ইথানে যে লাল সরাণ টো ছিল উটা পাক্কা হইয়ে গিছে। ঢালাই করা পিলেন সরাণ। তুয়ার যে ইস্কুলটো ছিল, উটা কি সুন্দর নীল সাদা রং হইয়েছে। ই গেরামের সব ছূটো ছাঁড়াগুলান ডিরেস পইরে সাইকেল লিয়ে ইস্কুল যায়। সরকার থিকে সব কোটাকে সাইকেল দিছে। কি সুন্দর চকচক্কে

নুতোন সাইকেল, ডিরেস দিছে। দুপুরে থাবার দিছে। বই দিছে, টাক্কাও দিছে। আক্কার বোইলছে বিটিগুলানের বিয়ার সময় পঞ্চিস হাজ্জার টাকাও দিবে। তু থাইকলে গোপাল হাইসদার বড় বিটিটার সাথে দু পাশে বিনুনি ঝুলায়ে নীল সাদা সাড়ি পোইড়ে ক্রীং ক্রীং বেল বাজ্জায়ে ইস্কুল যেতিস রে মা। কি জানি তু এখান বেইচে আছিস না মোইরে গিছিস। সীতামোণি আর আসে না গেরামে। তুয়ার থক্করও পাই না। তুয়ার ভাইটো কিলাস ইবার মাইদ্দোমিক দিবে। খুব মন দিয়ে পোইড়ছে। দিদির পার্টির লোক গুলান গেরামের ছেইলেগুলানরে পুলিশের চাকরী দিছে। লাল পার্টির মাতব্বরগুলান আর গিরামে ঢুকে না। সব পলাইছে। হুল পার্টির লোক গুলানকেও আর দেখিনা। জঙ্গল মহল শান্ত হোইয়ে গিছে। বোম লাই, গুলি লাই। মারামারি লাই। দিদির পার্টির লোকগুলান আমাকে আর তোর মাকে কাজ দিছে। পুকুর কাইটছি আমরা, সরান বানাইছ্ছি। গিরামে দুটা টিউকল দিছে। জল আইনতে আর দূরে যেইত্যে হয়েক লাই তুয়ার মাকে। ইখান আর অভাব লাই রে বিটি। তু ফিরে আয়। তুয়ারে কমলি ফুল মাতখায় গুইজ্যে দিব, চুলে ঠাইন্ডা তেল দিয়ে মাতখা আচড়াই দিবো, তুয়ার সাথে সানঝ নাইমলে গল্প কইরবো, তুয়াকে ফের লিজের হাতে থাওয়াই দিব মা। তু ফিরে আয় থালি। তুয়ার বাপ আর তুয়াকে বাবুদের বাড়ির বাসসোন ধুতে পাঠাবেক লাই রে মা, বাবুদের এঁটো থাক্কার থেতে দিবেক লাই। তুই চোইলি আয় রে মা, বাপটোর বুক ঠাইন্ডা কইরে দে মা। ইতি, তুয়ার থারাপ বাপ